ANNE WILLAN'S
LOOK&COOK

French Country Cooking

ANNE WILLAN'S
LOOK&COOK

French Country Cooking

Stoddart

A DORLING KINDERSLEY BOOK

Created and produced by
CARROLL & BROWN LIMITED
5 Lonsdale Road
London NW6 6RA

Project Editor Anne Crane
Assistant Editors Valerie Cipollone and Stella Vayne

Editorial Consultant Jeni Wright

Art Editor Alan Watt
Designers Sue Knight and Lucy De Rosa

Photographers David Murray and Jules Selmes

Production Wendy Rogers and Amanda Mackie

First published in Canada in 1995 by
Stoddart Publishing Co. Limited,
34 Lesmill Road, Toronto, Canada, M3B 2T6

Canadian Cataloguing in Publication data

Willan, Anne
French country cooking

(Anne Willan's look & cook)
Includes index.
ISBN 0-7737-2856-2

I. Cookery, French. I. Title. II Series: Willan,
Anne, Anne Willan's look & cook

TX719.W55 1995   641.5944   C94–932850–2

Reproduced by Colourscan, Singapore
Printed and bound in Italy by A. Mondadori, Verona

CONTENTS

FRENCH COUNTRY COOKING

THE LOOK & COOK APPROACH

Welcome to **French Country Cooking** and the *Look & Cook* series. These volumes are designed to be the simplest, most informative cookbooks you'll ever own. They are the closest I can come to sharing my personal techniques for cooking my own favorite recipes without actually being with you in the kitchen.

Equipment and ingredients often determine whether or not you can cook a particular dish, so *Look & Cook* illustrates everything you need at the beginning of each recipe. You'll see at a glance how long a recipe takes to cook, how many servings it makes, what the finished dish looks like, and how much preparation can be done ahead. When you start to cook, you'll find the preparation and cooking are organized into steps that are easy to follow. Each stage has its own color coding and everything is shown in photographs with brief text to go with each step. You will never be in doubt as to what it is you are doing, why you are doing it, and how it should look.

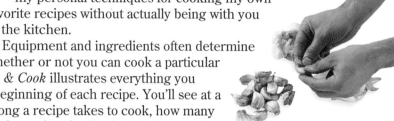

EQUIPMENT

INGREDIENTS

🍽 SERVES 4–6   🥘 WORK TIME 20–25 MINUTES   ☕ COOKING TIME 20–25 MINUTES

I've also included helpful hints and ideas under "Anne Says." These may list an alternative ingredient or piece of equipment, or explain a certain method, or add some advice on mastering a particular technique. Similarly, if there is a crucial stage in a recipe when things can go astray, I've included some warnings called "Take Care."

Many of the photographs are annotated to pinpoint why certain pieces of equipment work best, and how food should look at the various stages of cooking. Because presentation is so important, a picture of the finished dish with serving suggestions is at the end of each recipe.

Thanks to all this information, you can't go wrong. I'll be with you every step of the way. So please come with me into the kitchen to look, cook, and enjoy some delicious **French Country Cooking**.

Anne Willan

WHY FRENCH COUNTRY COOKING?

French country cooking survives triumphantly despite the vagaries of fashion. The combination of top-quality ingredients and traditional recipes has proved unbeatable time and time again. Consider cassoulet: pungent Languedoc sausage and garlic, plus the inspired addition of duck confit, transforms what would otherwise be little more than a pot of pork and baked beans. The humble bacon and egg pie, quiche Lorraine, has achieved world renown simply because French cooks insist on using full-flavored smoky bacon in the rich custard, and on prebaking the pastry shell so that it remains crisp. It is this attention to ingredients and technique that gives French country cooking its authority.

Even today, France can still lay claim to the world's finest ingredients. The Paris basin has long been known as France's breadbasket, while on the fertile soil of Burgundy to the south and the Loire to the west there are orchards and market gardens, pedigree beef cattle such as Charolais, and free-range chickens like those of Bresse, the aristocrats of the farmyard. Quality control of food began in France with the appellation controlée *status for wines, a concept which has since been extended to a range of foods, notably poultry and cheese.*

Brittany and the northern coastline offer superb fish and shellfish. In the south, the Mediterranean still furnishes specialties like spiny lobster and red mullet. Inland, especially in the mountains, there are dried hams and sausages, and fine cheeses.

In making the most of this material, simplicity is the key. Solo ingredients are orchestrated with vegetables, herbs, butter or oil, and wine or cider. Natural marriages abound. You find that small birds that live among the vines are cooked with vine leaves, while Gascon prunes marinated in local Armagnac form the basis of a sublime ice cream. Long slow simmering in a braise, soup, or stew is characteristic, and where would the French kitchen be without the stockpot?

As everywhere else, cooking is changing in rural France. The microwaved hamburger and the packaged pizza can now be found in the smallest village café. But that same village will have a baker who rises at 4 o'clock in the morning, six days a week, to produce crusty loaves for the breakfast table. In all but the largest cities, lunch remains the main meal of the day to be shared with the whole family, and three, even four, courses are routine. Supper holds true to its original meaning of soup, with perhaps an omelet or a slice of ham, and plenty of bread. Grand desserts, such as snow eggs, are reserved for weekends and feast days, as are the great classics of country cooking, such as duck with tart cherries. These are savored at leisure around the family table. You'll find a few of them in this book, together with a warming collection of the more everyday dishes that country cooks do so well. I hope you enjoy them all as much as I do.

RECIPE CHOICE

A French cook shops regularly at the local market, and plans the meal around the produce available. I like to do the same, preparing hearty meals laden with root vegetables in the winter, and serving tender vegetables, lighter greens, and salads as the weather warms in spring. In summer, choose recipes abundant in aromatic herbs and fresh fruit. Below is a summary of recipes you will find in this volume.

FIRST COURSES

Black Olive Dip with Crudités (La Grande Tapenade): a platter of crisp fresh vegetables is served with a pungent sauce of black olives puréed with capers, anchovies, and garlic. *Eggs Stuffed with Black Olive and Anchovy Sauce (Oeufs Durs en Tapenade)*: the olive sauce is mellowed with the addition of hard-boiled egg yolks, then piped into egg-white halves. *Warm Salad of Wild Mushrooms (Salade Tiède aux Champignons Sauvages)*: sautéed fresh wild mushrooms are set off with a salad of gourmet greens. *Warm Salad of Chicken Livers (Salade Tiède aux Foies de Volaille)*: pieces of sautéed chicken liver are teamed with gourmet salad greens. *Country Terrine (Terrine de Campagne)*: slices of this terrine reveal strips of ham running through a traditional forcemeat mixture of ground pork and veal flavored with brandy and spices. *Game Terrine (Terrine de Gibier)*: for an autumnal version of Country Terrine, ground venison replaces the veal.

MAIN DISHES AND ACCOMPANIMENTS

Quiche Lorraine: I like to add Gruyère cheese to this French classic of egg custard and bacon in a flaky pastry shell. *Leek and Cheese Quiche (Quiche aux Poireaux et Fromage)*: sliced leeks are cooked until soft, then baked in the egg custard with plenty of Gruyère cheese. *Buckwheat Crêpes with Seafood (Galettes de Sarrasin aux Fruits de Mer)*: nutty buckwheat crêpes are rolled around a creamy seafood mixture of shrimp, scallops, and sole. *Buckwheat Crêpes with Ham (Galettes de Sarrasin au Jambon)*:

the French version of a ham and cheese sandwich. *Omelet with Peppers and Tomatoes (Omelette Basquaise)*: a zesty combination of bell peppers, onions, and tomatoes, spiked with chili pepper, fills this flat omelet from southwestern France. *Country Omelet (Omelette Paysanne)*: cubes of potatoes, crisp bacon, and sliced onions fill this tasty omelet. *Scallops with Tomatoes, Garlic, and Herbs (Coquilles St. Jacques à la Provençale)*: sweet scallops are briskly cooked, then paired with a tomato and garlic *concassée*. *Spiced Scallops (Coquilles St. Jacques Nantaise)*: Nantes, once the spice port for the Orient, boasts this recipe of scallops flavored with curry spices, tomatoes, and onion. *Roast Sea Bass with Herb Butter Sauce (Loup Rôti au Beurre de Montpellier)*: sliced lemon and sprigs of fresh thyme stud a whole roasted sea bass. A Mediterranean combination of olive oil, anchovies, capers, garlic, and herbs features in the accompanying sauce. *Loire Sea Bass (Loup Rôti, Sauce Beurre Blanc)*: slightly acidic *beurre blanc* is the perfect balance to the mild roast sea bass. *Sweet-Sour Duck with Cherries (Canard aux Cerises à l'Aigre-doux)*: tangy cherries are the ideal foil to the rich flavor of crisp roast duck. *Duck with Pears (Canard aux Poires)*: roast duck is teamed with pear halves poached in red wine. *Cornish Hens in Grape Leaves (Coquelets à la Vigneronne)*: stuffed small birds keep moist when wrapped in vine leaves and sliced bacon. *Cornish Hens with Braised Belgian Endive (Coquelets aux Endives Braisées)*: braised Belgian endive accompanies stuffed small birds served with a sharp vinegar sauce. *Sauté of Chicken with Shrimp (Sauté de Poulet aux Crevettes)*: chicken and shrimp marry in this sauté from Burgundy. Tomatoes, white wine, chicken stock, and a splash of *marc de Bourgogne* add characteristic flavor. *Sauté of Chicken with Fennel (Sauté de Poulet au Fenouil)*: the anise flavor of fennel blends pleasantly with chicken as they cook together in this sauté. *Rabbit with Provençal Herbs and Baked Tomatoes (Lapin aux Herbes de Provence, Tomates au Four)*: a marinade of Provençal herbs, olive oil, and white wine doubles as the cooking liquid in this rabbit stew. Plum tomatoes are slowly baked until sweet and tender to serve with it. *Chicken with Provençal Herbs and Garlic Potatoes (Poulet aux Herbes de Provence, Pommes à l'Ail)*: chicken replaces the rabbit in this stew served with crisp garlic-flavored potatoes.

Cassoulet with Quick Confit: a hearty winter casserole – speedy duck confit, cubes of lamb, and country sausage are stewed with beans and tomatoes and topped with a golden crust. *Poor Man's Cassoulet*: cubes of pork replace the lamb in this simpler version of cassoulet. *Spring Lamb Stew (Navarin Printanier)*: in this distinctive stew, chunks of lamb are simmered in stock until just tender, then cooked with carrots, turnips, potatoes, baby onions, green beans, and peas. *Lamb Ratatouille (Ratatouille d'Agneau)*: bell pepper strips, eggplant, tomatoes, and onion form a ratatouille before combining with the lamb in this succulent stew. *Leg of Lamb with Roasted Garlic and Shallots (Gigot à l'Ail et aux Echalotes Rôtis)*: garlic cloves and whole shallots mellow and sweeten when they are roasted beside a leg of lamb. *Leg of Lamb with Potatoes (Gigot Boulangère)*: sliced potatoes and onion roast beneath a leg of lamb and absorb the tasty cooking juices. *Steak au Poivre*: crushed black peppercorns add heat to steak, and French fried potatoes are the perfect accompaniment. *Steak with White Wine and Shallots (Steak au Vin Blanc et Echalotes)*: individual steaks feature in this version of Steak au Poivre served with an intensely flavored white wine sauce and crunchy French fried potatoes. *Pork Chops with Mustard Sauce (Côtes de Porc Dijonnaise)*: a lively mustard sauce highlights tender pork chops. *Veal Chops with Mustard Sauce and Baby Onions (Côtes de Veau Dijonnaise aux Petits Oignons)*: the mustard sauce complements the mild flavor of veal with baby onions. *Zucchini Tian (Tian de Courgettes)*: in this Provençal specialty, chopped zucchini, garlic, and onion are baked with cooked rice and eggs. *Spinach and Mushroom Tian (Tian d'Epinards et Champignons)*: a tempting side dish of spinach and mushrooms flavored with grated Parmesan. *Creamy Scalloped Potatoes (Gratin Dauphinois)*: thinly sliced potatoes, cooked first in milk, then in heavy cream, are sprinkled with Gruyère cheese, and baked until bubbling – a rich and delicious accompaniment to any meal. *Gratin of Root Vegetables (Gratin de Racines d'Hiver)*: carrots brighten this rich version of Gratin Dauphinois.

DESSERTS

Cherry Clafoutis (Clafoutis aux Cerises): fresh cherries stud a baked batter pudding that is dusted with confectioners' sugar just before serving. *Plum Clafoutis (Clafoutis aux Prunes)*: purple plum halves are baked in batter. *Apricot and Hazelnut Ice Cream (Glace Auxerroise)*: dried apricots enhance the flavor, while chopped hazelnuts add crunch to vanilla ice cream. *Prune and Armagnac Ice Cream (Glace Gasconne)*: a Gascon favorite – vanilla ice cream is flecked with Armagnac soaked prunes. *Golden Rice Pudding with Peaches and Red Wine (Terrinée et Chicolle)*: fresh peaches macerated in red wine add an appealing contrast to this creamy rice pudding. *Rice Pudding with Dried Fruit Compote (Terrinée à la Confit de Fruits Secs)*: dried figs, apricots, and golden raisins are cooked with a clove to serve with a soft rice pudding. *Snow Eggs (Oeufs à la Neige)*: a caramel lattice decorates clouds of meringue floating on a pool of vanilla custard sauce. *Chocolate Snow Eggs (Oeufs à la Neige au Chocolat)*: semisweet chocolate darkens the custard sauce and decorates the meringues. *Rustic Apple Tart (Tarte aux Pommes Ménagère)*: an apple purée hides beneath a fan of apple slices in a pastry crust. *Apple Tartlets (Tartelettes aux Pommes)*: an elegant version of a classic dessert.

FRENCH COUNTRY MENUS

French country dining is often based on family meals. The midday meal, traditionally the day's largest, is usually served in several courses. It may open with a slice of pâté, slivers of dried sausage, or perhaps a salad of grated carrot. The main course will be chicken or meat, fish on Fridays, with a vegetable, followed by cheese, then fruit. The evening meal is much simpler, usually just one course.

Seasons and special occasions figure in menu planning as well. Summer is the season for lighter meals. For a casual evening among friends, Black Olive Dip with Crudités as an opener, and Roast Sea Bass with Herb Butter Sauce as a main course are both easy to prepare. Finish the meal with French cheeses and fresh fruit.

Plan an elegant dinner to show off autumn produce, and begin the meal with Warm Salad of Wild Mushrooms. Serve Cornish Hens in Grape Leaves to celebrate the grape harvest, followed by freshly baked Apple Tartlets, all accompanied by your favorite French wine, red or white.

Holiday meals deserve special attention as well as special ingredients. Start the meal with Scallops with Tomatoes, Garlic, and Herbs. The tomato garnish may be prepared in advance, but cook the scallops just before serving. Leg of Lamb with Roasted Garlic and Shallots warrants an equally distinctive accompaniment, like Zucchini Tian. For dessert, impress your family and friends with Snow Eggs floating in vanilla custard, topped with a golden caramel lattice and sliced almonds.

BLACK OLIVE DIP WITH CRUDITES

La Grande Tapenade

🍽 SERVES 6–8　　🥣 WORK TIME 30–35 MINUTES　　🍲 BAKING TIME 10–15 MINUTES

EQUIPMENT

chef's knife

small knife

vegetable peeler

food processor

olive pitter

bowls

rubber spatula

serrated knife

baking sheet

chopping board

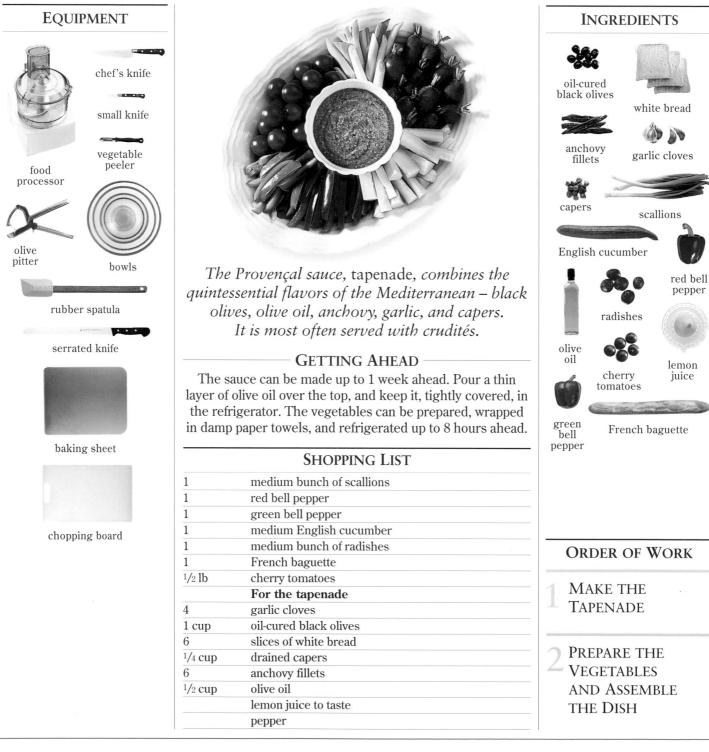

The Provençal sauce, tapenade, *combines the quintessential flavors of the Mediterranean – black olives, olive oil, anchovy, garlic, and capers. It is most often served with crudités.*

GETTING AHEAD

The sauce can be made up to 1 week ahead. Pour a thin layer of olive oil over the top, and keep it, tightly covered, in the refrigerator. The vegetables can be prepared, wrapped in damp paper towels, and refrigerated up to 8 hours ahead.

SHOPPING LIST

1	medium bunch of scallions
1	red bell pepper
1	green bell pepper
1	medium English cucumber
1	medium bunch of radishes
1	French baguette
1/2 lb	cherry tomatoes
	For the tapenade
4	garlic cloves
1 cup	oil-cured black olives
6	slices of white bread
1/4 cup	drained capers
6	anchovy fillets
1/2 cup	olive oil
	lemon juice to taste
	pepper

INGREDIENTS

oil-cured black olives

white bread

anchovy fillets

garlic cloves

capers

scallions

English cucumber

red bell pepper

radishes

olive oil

lemon juice

cherry tomatoes

green bell pepper

French baguette

ORDER OF WORK

1 **MAKE THE TAPENADE**

2 **PREPARE THE VEGETABLES AND ASSEMBLE THE DISH**

1 MAKE THE TAPENADE

If available, buy oil-cured black olives from Provence

Olive pitter makes removing pits easy

1 Set the flat side of the chef's knife on top of each garlic clove and strike it with your fist. Discard the skin.

2 Using the olive pitter, pit the olives and discard the pits.

3 With the serrated knife, trim and discard the crusts from the bread. Roughly tear the bread slices into pieces and place them in a medium bowl. Pour cold water over the slices to generously cover them. Leave to soak, 5 minutes.

4 Squeeze the bread dry with your fists and put the pieces into the food processor.

Olive oil is added in steady stream

5 Add the garlic cloves, olives, capers, and anchovy fillets to the food processor and chop coarsely. With the blades turning, gradually add the olive oil. Add lemon juice and pepper to taste, and work again briefly.

6 Transfer the tapenade to a bowl, scraping the side of the processor bowl with the rubber spatula. Cover, and set aside until ready to serve.

ANNE SAYS
"You can make a coarse or finely chopped mixture, as you prefer."

HOW TO CORE AND SEED A BELL PEPPER AND CUT IT INTO STRIPS OR DICE

The core and seeds of a bell pepper should be discarded before cutting the pepper into strips or dice.

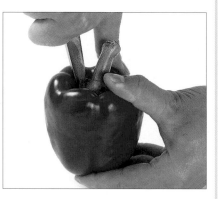

1 With a small knife, cut around the core of the bell pepper. Twist the core, and pull it out.

2 Halve the pepper lengthwise, and scrape out the seeds. Cut away the white ribs on the inside.

3 Set each pepper half cut-side down, flatten it with the heel of your hand, and, using a chef's knife, slice it lengthwise into strips. For dice, gather the strips together, and cut crosswise.

2 PREPARE THE VEGETABLES AND ASSEMBLE THE DISH

1 Trim the scallions and cut them into 2-inch pieces, including some of their green tops. Core and seed the red and green bell peppers and cut them into strips (see box, left).

2 Trim the ends off the cucumber with the chef's knife, then peel it with the vegetable peeler.

Cucumber seeds are discarded

3 Cut the cucumber lengthwise in half, then scoop out the seeds with a teaspoon.

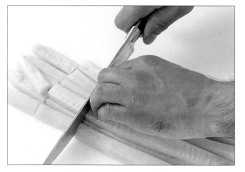

4 Cut the cucumber halves lengthwise into 2–3 strips, then gather the strips into a bundle and cut them crosswise into 2-inch pieces.

5 Using the small knife, trim the roots and tops of the radishes, leaving a little of the green tops.

After baking, bread should feel crisp

6 Heat the oven to 375°F. With the serrated knife, cut the bread into ¼-inch slices on the diagonal, discarding the ends. Set the slices on the baking sheet and bake in the heated oven until crisp and beginning to brown, 10–15 minutes.

🍴 TO SERVE

Transfer the tapenade to a small serving bowl and set it in the center of a large platter. Arrange the scallions, radishes, cucumber strips, bell pepper strips, and cherry tomatoes around the tapenade. Serve the toasted bread separately.

Tapenade is delicious accompaniment to aperitifs

Crisp bread and crudités both go well with tapenade

EGGS STUFFED WITH BLACK OLIVE AND ANCHOVY SAUCE

OEUFS DURS EN TAPENADE

In this Provençal version of deviled eggs, the yolks of hard-boiled eggs are blended with the tapenade mixture. The sauce can be made up to 1 week ahead, but cook the eggs the day of serving.

1 Omit the scallions, bell peppers, cucumber, radishes, French baguette, and cherry tomatoes. Make the tapenade as directed, omitting the bread and using 3 garlic cloves, ½ cup oil-cured black olives, 4 anchovy fillets, 2 tbsp drained capers, ⅓ cup olive oil, and pepper to taste. Cut 4 more anchovy fillets lengthwise in half, then cut each half crosswise into 3 pieces and set them aside for decoration.

2 Put 6 eggs into a saucepan of cold water, bring to a boil, and simmer, 10 minutes. Remove from the heat and run cold water into the pan to stop the eggs cooking. Allow to cool, then drain. Tap the eggs to crack the shells, then peel them, rinse with cold water, and pat dry.

3 Slice the eggs lengthwise in half, then separate the yolks from the whites. Put the yolks into a strainer set over a medium bowl and work them through with the back of a metal spoon. Scrape away the yolk clinging to the bottom of the strainer. Reserve 2 tbsp of the yolks for decoration, add the tapenade to the remaining yolks, and beat with a wooden spoon until well mixed.

4 Shortly before serving, stuff the egg whites: put the tapenade mixture into a pastry bag fitted with a large star tube and pipe rosettes into the egg whites. Alternatively, use a teaspoon to fill the egg whites. Top each half with a small spoonful of sieved egg yolk and an anchovy cross. Arrange the stuffed eggs on a platter and decorate with parsley sprigs. Serves 4–6.

WARM SALAD OF WILD MUSHROOMS

Salade Tiède aux Champignons Sauvages

🍴 SERVES 4 🥣 WORK TIME 25–30 MINUTES 🍲 COOKING TIME 8–10 MINUTES

EQUIPMENT

chef's knife

wooden spoon

small knife

whisk

large frying pan

bowls

salad spinner†

chopping board

paper towels

†dish towel can also be used

INGREDIENTS

vegetable oil

mixed wild mushrooms

red wine vinegar

radicchio

arugula

butter

parsley

walnut oil

shallots

Dijon-style mustard

curly endive

ANNE SAYS
"To make expensive wild mushrooms go further, you can replace half of them with button mushrooms."

Wild mushrooms are a true delicacy calling for the simplest preparation. A favorite first course is to sauté the mushrooms with chopped shallot and parsley and serve them on a bed of salad.

GETTING AHEAD
The vinaigrette dressing can be made up to 1 week in advance and kept in a sealed container. Prepare the salad leaves up to 1 day ahead and keep them, wrapped in a damp dish towel, in the refrigerator.

SHOPPING LIST

1	small head of curly endive, weighing about 1/4 lb
1	small head of radicchio, weighing about 2 1/2 oz
2 1/2 oz	arugula
3/4 lb	mixed wild mushrooms, such as chanterelles, oyster mushrooms, and cèpes
2	shallots
1	small bunch of parsley
2–3 tbsp	butter
	For the vinaigrette dressing
2 tbsp	red wine vinegar
1/2 tsp	Dijon-style mustard
	salt and pepper
3 tbsp	vegetable oil
3 tbsp	walnut oil

ORDER OF WORK

1 MAKE THE VINAIGRETTE DRESSING AND WASH THE GREENS

2 PREPARE THE MUSHROOMS AND ASSEMBLE THE SALAD

1 MAKE THE VINAIGRETTE DRESSING AND WASH THE GREENS

1 Make the vinaigrette dressing (see box, below). Pull the curly endive leaves apart and discard the tough stems. Tear the leaves into pieces and immerse them in plenty of cold water.

2 Discard any withered outer leaves from the radicchio and cut away the core. Separate the leaves and immerse them with the curly endive.

All salad leaves are washed together

3 Discard the tough stems from the arugula and immerse the leaves in the bowl of cold water.

Tough stems are removed before leaves are washed

4 Wash the endive, radicchio, and arugula leaves thoroughly. Dry the leaves in the salad spinner or on a dish towel, then transfer all the leaves to a large bowl.

HOW TO MAKE VINAIGRETTE DRESSING

The standard recipe for vinaigrette dressing follows the principle of 1 part vinegar to 3 parts oil, but these quantities can vary according to taste, the type of vinegar and oil, and the other ingredients used.

In a bowl, whisk together the vinegar, mustard, and salt and pepper. Gradually whisk in the vegetable and walnut oils so the vinaigrette emulsifies and thickens slightly. Taste for seasoning.

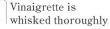

Vinaigrette is whisked thoroughly

2 PREPARE THE MUSHROOMS AND ASSEMBLE THE SALAD

1 Wipe the wild mushrooms with damp paper towels. Wash them only if they are very sandy, and do not let them soak in water. Trim the stems and remove woody portions.

Woody parts of mushrooms are cut away

2 Place the mushrooms on a chopping board and cut them into medium pieces with the chef's knife.

3 Peel the shallots, leaving a little of the root attached, and cut them in half. Set each half, flat-side down, on the chopping board and slice horizontally, leaving the slices attached at the root. Slice vertically, again leaving the root end uncut, then cut across the shallot to make fine dice.

Parsley sprigs are stripped by hand

4 Strip the parsley leaves from the stems and pile the leaves on the chopping board. With the chef's knife, finely chop them.

5 Heat the butter in the frying pan until foaming. Add the shallots and cook, stirring occasionally, until soft, 2–3 minutes.

6 Add the mushrooms and salt and pepper. Cook, stirring, until the mushrooms are tender and all the liquid has evaporated, 5–7 minutes. Stir in the chopped parsley and taste for seasoning.

Parsley is added when mushrooms are almost cooked

7 Briskly whisk the vinaigrette to re-emulsify it, then pour it over the salad leaves and toss them until coated. Taste for seasoning.

! TAKE CARE !
If the salad leaves are tossed in the vinaigrette too far in advance they will wilt.

🍽 TO SERVE
Divide the salad leaves among 4 individual plates. Spoon over the mushrooms. Serve at once, while the salad leaves are crisp and the mushrooms still warm.

Wild mushrooms have exceptional flavor

Salad leaves can be varied according to taste

WARM SALAD OF CHICKEN LIVERS

SALADE TIEDE AUX FOIES DE VOLAILLE

Chicken livers, cooked with a touch of red wine vinegar, take the place of wild mushrooms in this bistro-style salad.

1 Omit the wild mushrooms and parsley. Make the vinaigrette dressing and prepare the salad leaves as directed. Using a small knife, trim any membrane from 4 chicken livers (total weight about 1/4 lb), then cut each liver into 3 pieces. Coarsely chop the leaves from 5–7 sprigs of fresh tarragon.
2 Toss the salad leaves in the vinaigrette dressing, then arrange them on 4 individual plates.
3 Melt 2 tbsp butter in a frying pan, add the shallots, and sauté until soft. Add the chicken livers and salt and pepper. Fry the livers over high heat, shaking the pan occasionally, until brown on the outside, 1–2 minutes.
4 Add 2 tbsp red wine vinegar and bring to a boil, stirring to dissolve the pan juices. Stir in the chopped tarragon. Spoon 3 pieces of chicken liver with some pan juices onto each plate of salad.
Serve at once.

COUNTRY TERRINE

Terrine de Campagne

🍴 SERVES 8–10   🥣 WORK TIME 35–40 MINUTES*   🍲 COOKING TIME 1¼–1½ HOURS

EQUIPMENT

large terrine with lid (about 12 x 3 x 3 inches)

medium frying pan

roasting pan

paper towels

bowls

chef's knife

metal spatula

medium saucepan

large metal spoon

wooden spoon

strainer

small knife

metal skewer

chopping board

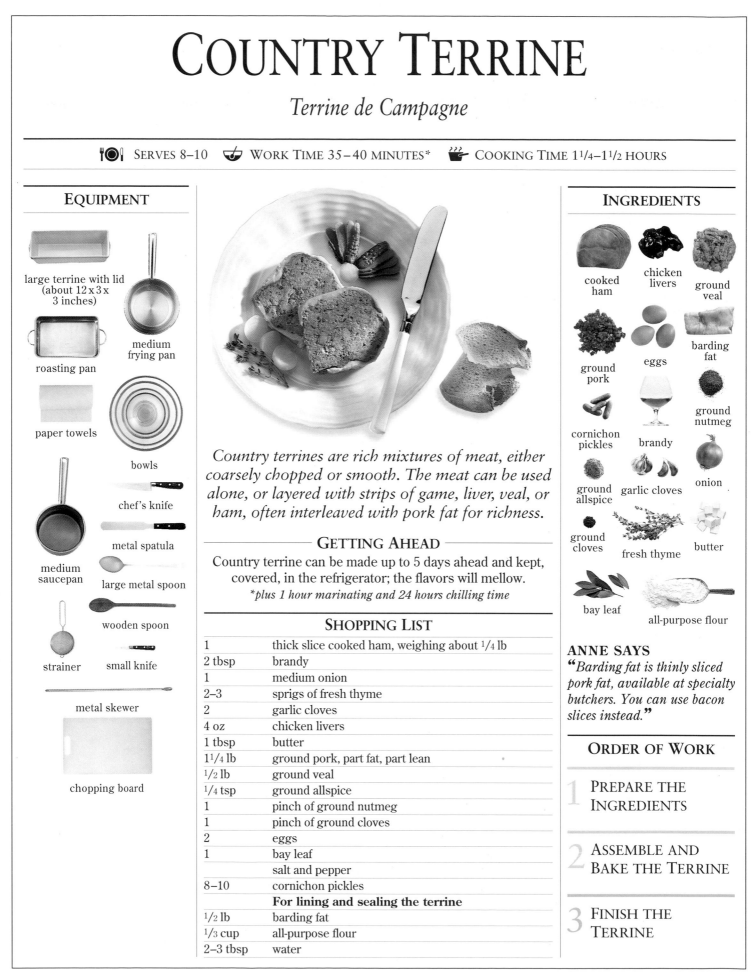

Country terrines are rich mixtures of meat, either coarsely chopped or smooth. The meat can be used alone, or layered with strips of game, liver, veal, or ham, often interleaved with pork fat for richness.

GETTING AHEAD

Country terrine can be made up to 5 days ahead and kept, covered, in the refrigerator; the flavors will mellow.

plus 1 hour marinating and 24 hours chilling time

SHOPPING LIST

1	thick slice cooked ham, weighing about ¼ lb
2 tbsp	brandy
1	medium onion
2–3	sprigs of fresh thyme
2	garlic cloves
4 oz	chicken livers
1 tbsp	butter
1¼ lb	ground pork, part fat, part lean
½ lb	ground veal
¼ tsp	ground allspice
1	pinch of ground nutmeg
1	pinch of ground cloves
2	eggs
1	bay leaf
	salt and pepper
8–10	cornichon pickles
	For lining and sealing the terrine
½ lb	barding fat
⅓ cup	all-purpose flour
2–3 tbsp	water

INGREDIENTS

cooked ham

chicken livers

ground veal

ground pork

eggs

barding fat

cornichon pickles

brandy

ground nutmeg

ground allspice

garlic cloves

onion

ground cloves

fresh thyme

butter

bay leaf

all-purpose flour

ANNE SAYS

"*Barding fat is thinly sliced pork fat, available at specialty butchers. You can use bacon slices instead.*"

ORDER OF WORK

1 PREPARE THE INGREDIENTS

2 ASSEMBLE AND BAKE THE TERRINE

3 FINISH THE TERRINE

1 PREPARE THE INGREDIENTS

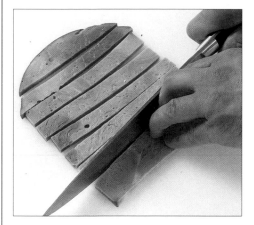

1 Place the slice of cooked ham on the chopping board and, using the chef's knife, slice it into long strips about ³/8-inch wide.

2 Combine the ham, brandy, and salt and pepper in a bowl. Cover, and let marinate, 1 hour. Meanwhile, prepare the remaining ingredients.

3 Peel the onion, leaving a little of the root attached and cut it lengthwise in half. Lay each onion half flat on the chopping board and slice horizontally toward the root, leaving the slices attached at the root end. Then slice vertically, again leaving the root end uncut. Finally, cut across the onion to make dice. Continue chopping the onion until it is very fine.

4 Strip the thyme leaves from the stems. Peel and finely chop the garlic cloves (see box, right). Trim any membrane from the chicken livers, and coarsely chop them.

Chicken liver adds rich flavor to terrine

HOW TO PEEL AND CHOP GARLIC

The strength of garlic varies with its age and dryness; use more when it is very fresh.

1 To separate the cloves, crush the bulb with the heel of your hand or pull a clove from the bulb with your fingers. To peel the clove, lightly crush it with the flat side of a chef's knife to loosen the skin.

2 Peel the skin from the garlic clove with your fingers.

3 To crush the clove, set the flat side of the knife on top and strike firmly with your fist. Finely chop the garlic with the knife, rocking the blade back and forth.

5 Melt the butter in the frying pan, add the onion, and cook, stirring occasionally, until soft and brown, 3–5 minutes. Turn into a bowl; let cool.

6 Add the garlic, thyme, chicken livers, ground pork, ground veal, allspice, nutmeg, cloves, and salt and pepper. Mix with a wooden spoon.

7 Crack the eggs into a bowl. Using a fork, beat the eggs to mix, then add them to the meat mixture.

Ham strips are flavored with brandy marinade

Mixture is combination of pork, veal, herbs, and spices

8 Strain the marinade from the ham into the mixture. With the wooden spoon, beat the mixture until it draws from the side of the bowl, 1–2 minutes.

9 Wipe the frying pan with paper towels. Add a little of the meat mixture and fry until browned on both sides, 1–2 minutes. Taste, and add more spices and salt and pepper if needed.

ANNE SAYS
"The mixture should be quite spicy."

2 ASSEMBLE AND BAKE THE TERRINE

2 Spoon half of the meat mixture into the terrine, then arrange the ham strips lengthwise, end to end, on the top.

Piece of barding fat is reserved to top meat mixture

1 Heat the oven to 350°F. Set aside 1 piece of barding fat and use the rest to line the bottom and longer sides of the terrine mold.

Overhanging barding fat will be folded over top of terrine before baking

3 Spread the remaining meat mixture over the ham, fold over the barding fat overhanging the sides of the terrine, then top with the reserved barding fat and the bay leaf. Cover the terrine with the lid.

Meat mixture is spread evenly over ham strips

4 Put the flour and water into a small bowl and mix together to make a soft smooth paste.

5 Using your fingers, seal the gap between the rim of the mold and the lid with the paste.

6 Set the mold in the roasting pan. Add boiling water to come halfway up the sides. Bring this water bath to a boil on top of the stove, then transfer the terrine in the pan to the oven.

7 Bake the terrine until the metal skewer inserted into the terrine for 30 seconds is hot to the touch when withdrawn, 1¼–1½ hours. Remove the terrine from the water bath and let it cool to tepid.

8 Remove the lid, cover the terrine, and set a weight on top. Chill for at least 1 day to allow the flavors to mellow.

ANNE SAYS
"A 1-lb weight is just heavy enough to compress the terrine so it slices well."

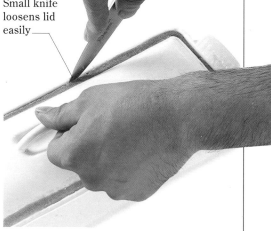

Small knife loosens lid easily

3 FINISH THE TERRINE

1 Cut each cornichon pickle lengthwise into 4–5 slices, leaving them attached at the stem ends.

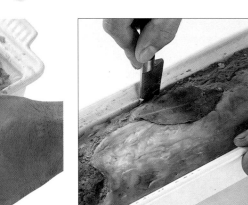

Fan shapes are pretty alternative to whole cornichons

Press lightly on cornichons to flatten them

2 Using your thumb or finger and thumb, flatten each cornichon pickle to make it into a fan shape.

3 With a metal spoon, scrape away and discard any fat from the top of the terrine.

Hardened fat is easy to remove

4 Dip a small knife into hot water and run it around the sides of the terrine to make it easier to turn out.

6 Using the chef's knife, cut the terrine into slices about 3/8-inch thick.

Slice carefully so terrine does not crumble

5 Holding the terrine mold with both hands, turn out the terrine onto a chopping board.

7 Arrange the terrine slices on individual plates or a large platter and decorate with the cornichons.

Use metal spatula to transfer cornichon fans

🍽 TO SERVE
Serve the terrine with pickled onions and crusty bread, if you like.

Barding fat is discarded before eating

Terrine can be served slightly chilled or at room temperature

GAME TERRINE

TERRINE DE GIBIER

Venison replaces the ground veal in this terrine, popular in the fall when hunting is a favorite French pastime. If venison is not available, you can replace it with the same weight of ground pheasant or rabbit.

1 Omit the ham, ground veal, and cornichon pickles. Cut a 1/4 lb piece of venison into strips 3/8-inch wide. With the flat side of a chef's knife, crush 3 juniper berries. Combine the juniper berries, brandy, and salt and pepper in a bowl. Add the venison strips and marinate as directed for the ham.

2 Make the meat mixture as directed, using 1/2 lb ground venison in place of the veal and adding 1/2 cup shelled pistachio nuts with the ground meat. Cook a small portion of the meat mixture, then taste for seasoning.

3 Assemble the terrine, lining the mold with 1/2 lb bacon slices instead of the barding fat and replacing the ham with the venison strips. Bake and unmold the terrine as directed.

QUICHE LORRAINE

🍽 SERVES 6 　🥄 WORK TIME 45–50 MINUTES* 　♨ BAKING TIME 30–35 MINUTES

EQUIPMENT

chef's knife

whisk

10-inch tart pan with removable base

ladle

rolling pin

slotted spoon

pastry brush

medium frying pan

scissors

bowls

paper towels

wire rack

strainer

baking sheet

grater

plastic wrap

pastry scraper

aluminum foil

dried beans or rice

INGREDIENTS

thick-cut bacon slices

Gruyère cheese

egg yolks

all-purpose flour

ground nutmeg

light cream

eggs

unsalted butter

ANNE SAYS
"For a lighter filling, replace half of the cream with milk."

Quiche, now known in many variations throughout the world, comes from the Lorraine in eastern France. Purists say it should be flavored only with bacon, but I like to add some grated Gruyère cheese. Serve it warm or at room temperature but never very hot as the custard will be too soft.

GETTING AHEAD
The pâte brisée dough can be made up to 2 days ahead and kept, tightly wrapped, in the refrigerator. The quiche is best on the day of baking.
plus 45 minutes chilling time

SHOPPING LIST

1/2 lb	thick-cut bacon slices
2 1/2 oz	Gruyère cheese
	For the pâte brisée dough
1 1/2 cups	all-purpose flour, more for work surface
1	egg yolk
1/2 tsp	salt
3 tbsp	water, more if needed
6 tbsp	unsalted butter, more for tart pan
	For the custard
2 cups	light cream
1	pinch of ground nutmeg
	salt and pepper
1	egg yolk
3	eggs

ORDER OF WORK

1 MAKE THE PATE BRISEE DOUGH

2 LINE THE TART PAN

3 BLIND BAKE THE PASTRY SHELL

4 MAKE THE FILLING AND BAKE THE QUICHE

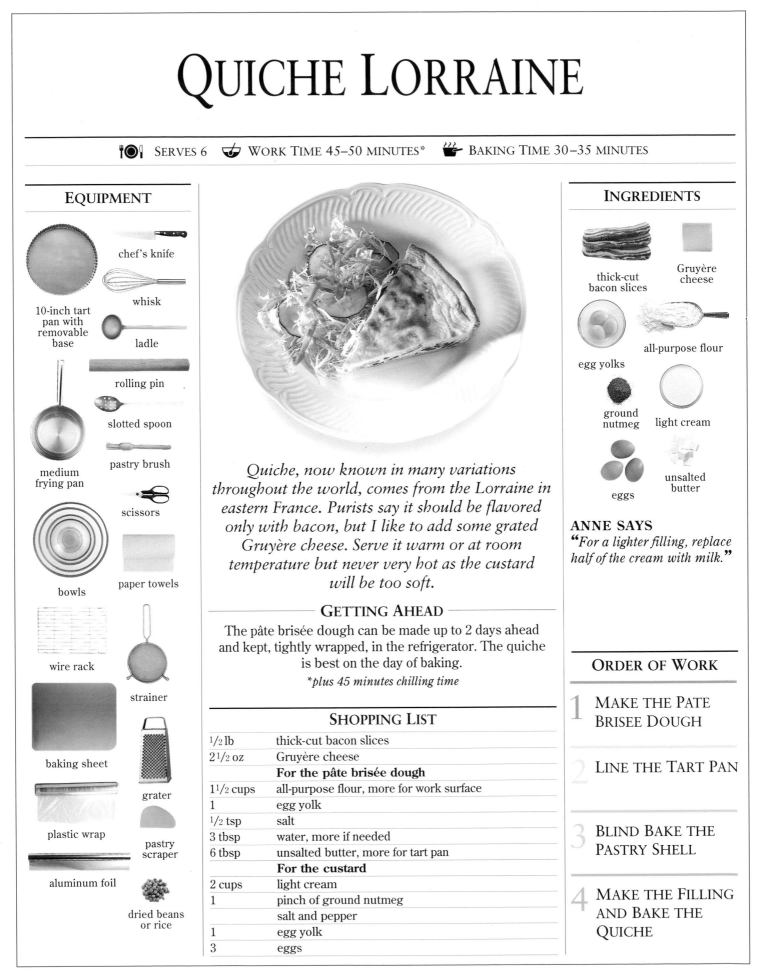

1 MAKE THE PATE BRISEE DOUGH

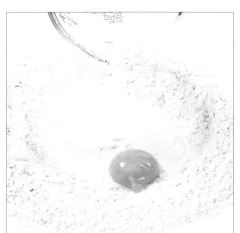

1 Sift the flour onto the work surface and make a well in the center. Put the egg yolk, salt, and water into the well.

2 Using the rolling pin, pound the butter to soften it slightly, then add it to the well in the flour. With your fingertips, work the ingredients in the well until thoroughly mixed.

Fingertips are ideal for mixing

3 Draw in the flour with the pastry scraper. With your fingers, work the flour into the other ingredients until coarse crumbs form. Press the dough into a ball.

ANNE SAYS
"If the crumbs are dry, sprinkle them with a little more water before pressing the dough together."

Knead dough until it is very pliable

4 Lightly flour the work surface, then blend the dough by pushing it away from you with the heel of your hand. Gather it up with the pastry scraper and continue to blend until it is very smooth and peels away from the work surface in one piece, 1–2 minutes.

5 Shape the dough into a ball, wrap it tightly in plastic wrap, and chill until firm, about 30 minutes.

2 LINE THE TART PAN

Dough is easy to lift when wrapped around rolling pin

1 Brush the tart pan with melted butter. Lightly flour the work surface. Roll out the chilled dough into a 12-inch round. Wrap the dough around the rolling pin and drape it over the pan, so that it hangs over the edge.

! TAKE CARE !
Be careful not to stretch the dough or it will shrink when baked.

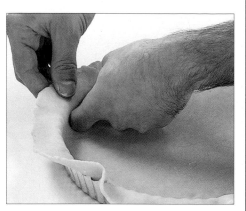

2 Gently lift the edge of the dough with one hand and press it well into the bottom edge of the pan with the forefinger of the other hand.

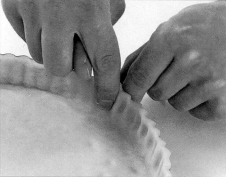

3 Roll the rolling pin over the top of the pan, pressing down to cut off the excess dough.

4 With your forefingers and thumb, press the dough evenly up the side, from the bottom, to increase the height of the dough shell.

5 Prick the bottom of the shell lightly with a fork to prevent air bubbles from forming during baking. Chill until firm, at least 15 minutes.

3 BLIND BAKE THE PASTRY SHELL

Dried chick peas are good for blind baking

Double thickness of foil helps dough keep its shape during baking

1 Heat the oven to 400°F. Put the baking sheet into the oven to heat. Line the pastry shell with a double thickness of foil, pressing it well into the bottom edge. Trim the foil if necessary, using the scissors, so that it stands about 1 1/2 inches above the edge of the pan.

2 Spread a layer of dried beans or rice over the foil to weigh down the dough while it is baking.

3 Place the tart pan on the baking sheet and bake the pastry shell in the heated oven until set and the rim starts to brown, about 10 minutes. Remove the foil and beans or rice.

4 Reduce the oven temperature to 375°F. Continue baking until the pastry is lightly browned, 5–8 minutes longer. Remove the pastry shell from the oven and let cool slightly. Leave the oven on at the same temperature.

4 MAKE THE FILLING AND BAKE THE QUICHE

Paper towels absorb excess fat from bacon

Bacon should be soft, not crispy

1 Stack the bacon slices on a chopping board and cut them crosswise into 1/4-inch strips.

2 Put the bacon into the frying pan, and cook, stirring occasionally, until lightly browned, 3–4 minutes.

3 Using the slotted spoon, lift the bacon out of the frying pan and transfer to paper towels to drain.

4 Put the cream, nutmeg, and salt and pepper into a bowl. Add the egg yolk and eggs and whisk until thoroughly mixed.

Custard is seasoned well with salt and pepper

5 Using the coarse side of the grater, grate the Gruyère cheese onto a plate and set aside.

6 Sprinkle the bacon pieces and grated cheese evenly over the bottom of the pastry shell.

7 Set the tart pan on the baking sheet. Whisk the custard mixture and ladle it over the bacon and cheese. Bake the quiche in the heated oven until lightly browned and the custard is set, 30–35 minutes.

ANNE SAYS

"*If the top is not brown, heat the broiler and broil the quiche if you like, 1–2 minutes. If the custard gets too brown during baking, cover the quiche loosely with a piece of foil.*"

Heating baking sheet ensures quiche bakes crisply

Bacon and cheese are covered with even layer of custard

8 Let the quiche cool slightly on the wire rack, then set the tart pan on a bowl to loosen and remove the side. Transfer the quiche to a chopping board or serving platter.

🍴 TO SERVE

Serve the quiche, cut into wedges, warm or at room temperature. Accompany with a salad, if you like.

LEEK AND CHEESE QUICHE

QUICHE AUX POIREAUX ET FROMAGE

Leeks are the only green vegetable found in our garden during the long Burgundian winter. I like to cook them until tender, then bake them in this quiche flavored with cheese.

1 Omit the bacon slices. Make the pâte brisée dough, line the tart pan, and blind bake the pastry shell as directed. Leave the oven on.

Gruyère-flavored custard is soft and golden

2 Trim 4 medium leeks (total weight about 3/4 lb), discarding the roots and tough green tops. With a chef's knife, slit the leeks lengthwise in half and wash them thoroughly under cold running water. Place each half, cut-side down, on a chopping board. Fan the leek slightly so that it lies flat, then cut each leek crosswise into 1/2-inch slices.

3 Heat 2 tbsp butter in a frying pan. Add the leeks and season with salt and pepper. Press a piece of buttered foil on top of the leeks and cover with a lid. Cook the leeks over very low heat, stirring occasionally, until they are very soft, 20–25 minutes. Do not allow the leeks to brown.

4 Heat the baking sheet as directed. Make the custard and grate 3 oz Gruyère cheese as directed. With a slotted spoon, transfer the sliced leeks to the pastry shell. Set the tart pan on the heated baking sheet, and ladle the custard over the leeks. Sprinkle with the grated cheese and bake the quiche as directed.

Seasonal salad is the classic partner for a slice of Quiche Lorraine

BUCKWHEAT CREPES WITH SEAFOOD

Galettes de Sarrasin aux Fruits de Mer

🍽 SERVES 6   🥣 WORK TIME 45–50 MINUTES   🍲 BAKING TIME 15–20 MINUTES

EQUIPMENT

chef's knife

metal spatula

small ladle

8-inch crêpe pan

whisk

slotted spoon

paper towels

small knife

pastry brush

baking dish

wooden spoon   strainer

bowls

colander

saucepans, 1 with lid, 1 heavy-based

chopping board

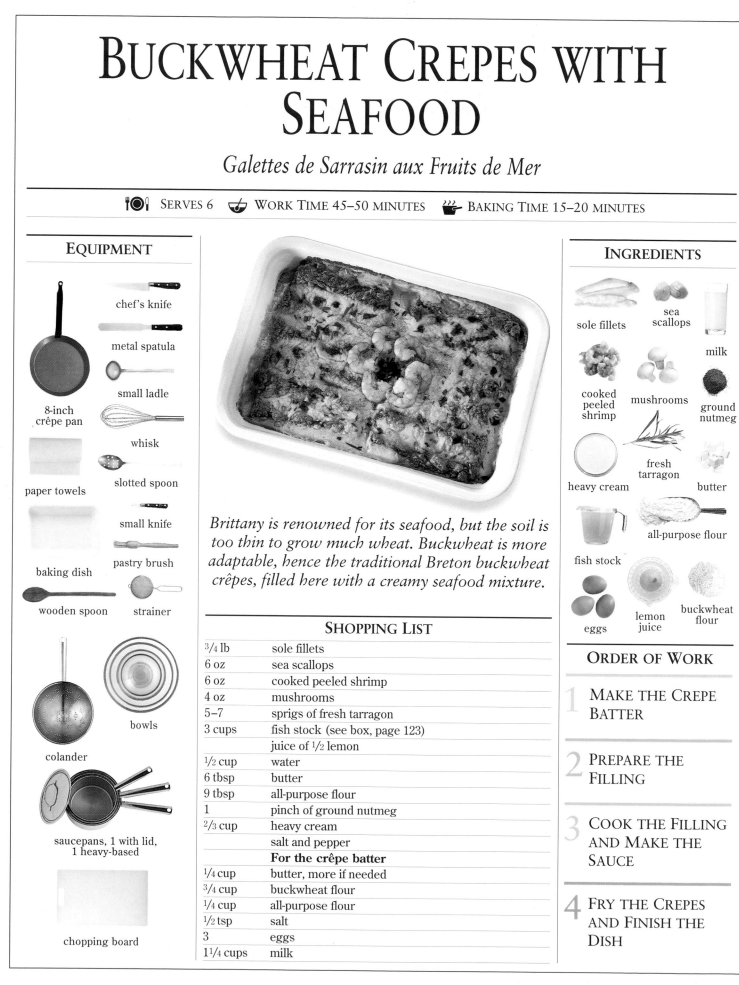

Brittany is renowned for its seafood, but the soil is too thin to grow much wheat. Buckwheat is more adaptable, hence the traditional Breton buckwheat crêpes, filled here with a creamy seafood mixture.

INGREDIENTS

sole fillets

sea scallops

milk

cooked peeled shrimp

mushrooms

ground nutmeg

heavy cream

fresh tarragon

butter

fish stock

all-purpose flour

eggs

lemon juice

buckwheat flour

SHOPPING LIST

¾ lb	sole fillets
6 oz	sea scallops
6 oz	cooked peeled shrimp
4 oz	mushrooms
5–7	sprigs of fresh tarragon
3 cups	fish stock (see box, page 123)
	juice of ½ lemon
½ cup	water
6 tbsp	butter
9 tbsp	all-purpose flour
1	pinch of ground nutmeg
⅔ cup	heavy cream
	salt and pepper
	For the crêpe batter
¼ cup	butter, more if needed
¾ cup	buckwheat flour
¼ cup	all-purpose flour
½ tsp	salt
3	eggs
1¼ cups	milk

ORDER OF WORK

1 MAKE THE CREPE BATTER

2 PREPARE THE FILLING

3 COOK THE FILLING AND MAKE THE SAUCE

4 FRY THE CREPES AND FINISH THE DISH

1 MAKE THE CREPE BATTER

1 Melt the butter in a small saucepan and set aside to cool. Sift both of the flours and the salt into a bowl.

2 Make a well in the center of the flour, add the eggs, and whisk until they are thoroughly mixed.

3 Pour half of the milk into the mixture in a slow, steady stream, whisking constantly and gradually drawing in the flour to make a smooth batter. Stir in half of the melted butter and half of the remaining milk. Cover the batter and let stand, 30 minutes. Meanwhile, prepare the filling.

Milk is added gradually so that no lumps form in batter

2 PREPARE THE FILLING

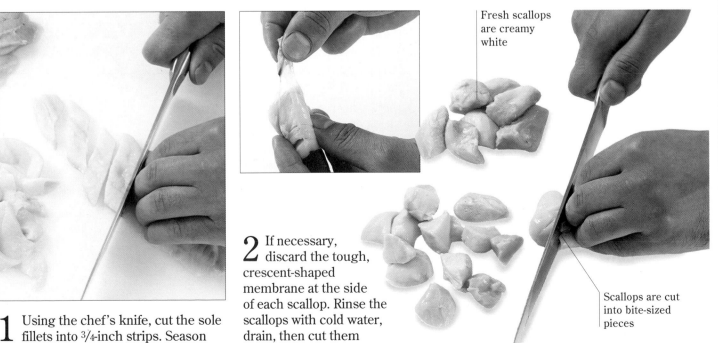

Fresh scallops are creamy white

Scallops are cut into bite-sized pieces

1 Using the chef's knife, cut the sole fillets into ¾-inch strips. Season the fish with salt and pepper.

2 If necessary, discard the tough, crescent-shaped membrane at the side of each scallop. Rinse the scallops with cold water, drain, then cut them into quarters.

3 Reserve 6 shrimp for decoration. Cut the remaining shrimp lengthwise and then crosswise in half. Put the quartered shrimp into a bowl.

4 Wipe the mushroom caps with damp paper towels and trim the stems even with the caps. Set the caps stem-side down and cut into quarters.

5 Strip the tarragon leaves from the stems and pile the leaves on the chopping board. Coarsely chop them with the chef's knife.

3 COOK THE FILLING AND MAKE THE SAUCE

1 In a medium saucepan, bring the fish stock to a boil. Add the sole strips and simmer until they just flake easily with a fork, 1–2 minutes.

Sole breaks into smaller pieces after cooking

Once cooked, fish becomes opaque

2 Lift out the sole strips with the slotted spoon and add them to the bowl with the shrimp.

3 Add the scallops to the fish stock. Simmer just until tender, 1–2 minutes. Transfer the scallops to the bowl of fish. Reserve the stock.

4 Put the mushrooms, lemon juice, water, and salt and pepper in a medium saucepan. Cover, and cook over high heat until the liquid boils to the top of the pan and the mushrooms are tender, 3–5 minutes.

5 With the slotted spoon, transfer the mushrooms to the bowl of seafood. Add their cooking liquid to the fish stock.

Mushroom cooking liquid is full of flavor

6 Make the sauce: melt the butter in the heavy-based saucepan over medium heat. Whisk in the flour and cook until foaming, 30–60 seconds.

7 Take the saucepan from the heat, let cool slightly, then strain in the fish stock and whisk to mix.

Sauce binds seafood and mushrooms

8 Return the saucepan to the heat and cook, whisking constantly, until the sauce boils and thickens. Season with the nutmeg, and salt and pepper to taste. Simmer the sauce until it is well flavored and thickly coats the back of a spoon, about 5 minutes.

9 Add half of the sauce to the seafood mixture. Reserve 1 tbsp of the chopped tarragon for decoration, add the rest to the mixture, and stir until combined. Taste for seasoning. Set the remaining sauce aside while frying the crêpes.

4 FRY THE CREPES AND FINISH THE DISH

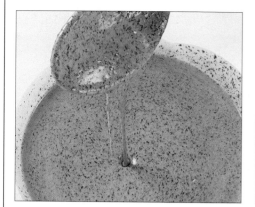

1 Using the wooden spoon, stir enough of the remaining milk into the batter to make it the consistency of thin cream. Brush the baking dish with melted butter.

2 Add the remaining melted butter to the crêpe pan and heat gently. Pour the excess into a bowl, leaving a thin film. Add a little batter and wait to see if it sputters, showing the pan is hot.

3 Pour in a small ladle of batter, rotating and shaking the pan at the same time so that the batter coats the bottom evenly and completely.

Lift crêpe with metal spatula

4 Fry the crêpe quickly over medium heat until it is set on top and brown underneath, 1–2 minutes. Loosen it with the metal spatula and toss or turn it. Continue cooking until brown on the other side, 30–60 seconds. Transfer the crêpe to a plate.

5 Continue with the remaining batter, adding more melted butter to the pan as necessary, to make a total of 12 crêpes. Pile the crêpes on top of each other on the plate.

Crêpes are stacked in neat pile so they stay moist and warm

6 Heat the oven to 350°F. Put about 2 tbsp of the filling into the center of each crêpe, fold in 2 sides, and roll up into a neat cylinder. Arrange seam-side down in the baking dish.

Roll up crêpe starting with unfolded side

7 Add the cream to the remaining sauce and bring to a boil, stirring constantly. Taste for seasoning.

8 Pour the sauce over the crêpes so they are completely coated. Bake the crêpes in the heated oven until the filling is hot and the sauce is bubbling, 15–20 minutes.

Sauce coats crêpes so they stay moist during baking

❢◉❢ TO SERVE

Arrange the 6 reserved shrimp in the middle of the dish, and sprinkle with the reserved tarragon. Serve at once, directly from the baking dish, allowing 2 crêpes per person.

Shrimp garnish echoes seafood filling

Sauce turns golden brown during baking

V A R I A T I O N

BUCKWHEAT CREPES WITH HAM

GALETTES DE SARRASIN AU JAMBON

Ham and cheese replace the seafood filling in this version of buckwheat crêpes.

1 Omit the seafood filling and sauce. Brush 6 individual gratin dishes with butter. Make the buckwheat crêpes as directed. Replace the seafood mixture with 1/2 lb thinly sliced cooked ham. Coarsely grate 1/2 lb Gruyère cheese. Reserve 1/4 cup of the grated cheese for topping.

2 Arrange a slice of cooked ham on a crêpe, then sprinkle it with 1–2 tbsp of the grated cheese. Fold the crêpe in half, then in half again to form a triangle. Repeat for the remaining crêpes.

3 Put 2 crêpes into each gratin dish and bake in the heated oven until hot, 10–15 minutes. Sprinkle the remaining cheese on top of each serving and bake the crêpes just until the cheese is melted, 3–5 minutes.

GETTING AHEAD

The crêpes can be made up to 2 days ahead, layered with waxed paper, and kept, tightly wrapped, in the refrigerator. The dish can be assembled up to 12 hours ahead and kept in the refrigerator, or it can be frozen. Bake it just before serving.

OMELET WITH PEPPERS AND TOMATOES

Omelette Basquaise

¶❍¶ SERVES 2   🥣 WORK TIME 20–25 MINUTES   ☕ COOKING TIME 15–25 MINUTES

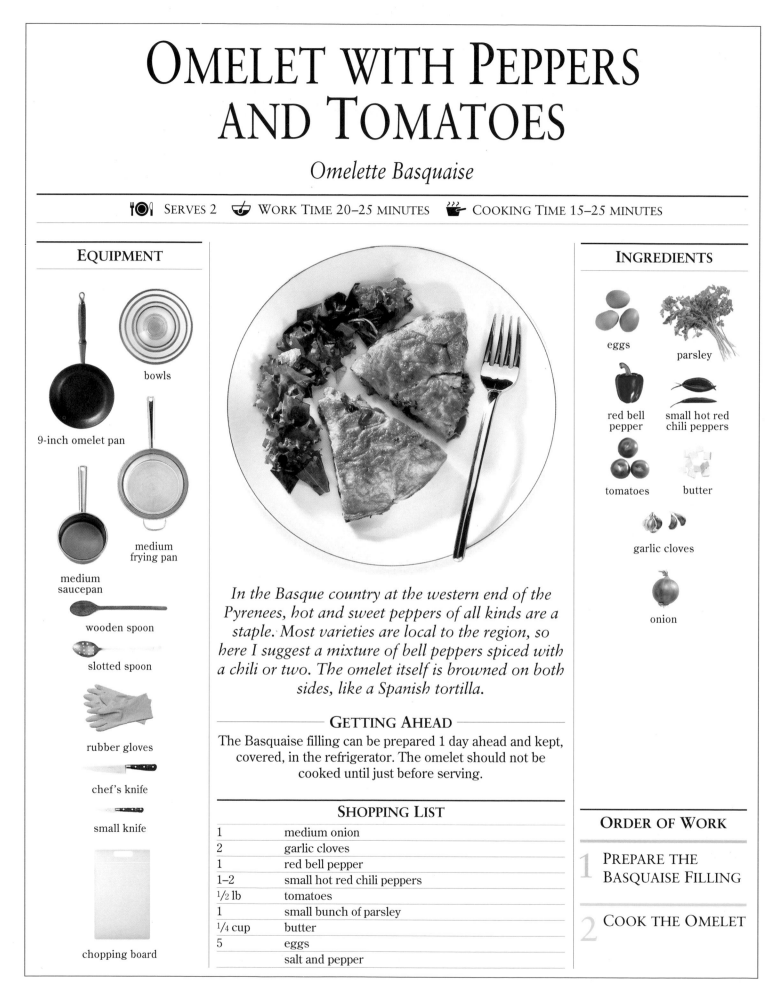

EQUIPMENT

bowls

9-inch omelet pan

medium frying pan

medium saucepan

wooden spoon

slotted spoon

rubber gloves

chef's knife

small knife

chopping board

INGREDIENTS

eggs

parsley

red bell pepper

small hot red chili peppers

tomatoes

butter

garlic cloves

onion

In the Basque country at the western end of the Pyrenees, hot and sweet peppers of all kinds are a staple. Most varieties are local to the region, so here I suggest a mixture of bell peppers spiced with a chili or two. The omelet itself is browned on both sides, like a Spanish tortilla.

GETTING AHEAD

The Basquaise filling can be prepared 1 day ahead and kept, covered, in the refrigerator. The omelet should not be cooked until just before serving.

SHOPPING LIST

1	medium onion
2	garlic cloves
1	red bell pepper
1–2	small hot red chili peppers
1/2 lb	tomatoes
1	small bunch of parsley
1/4 cup	butter
5	eggs
	salt and pepper

ORDER OF WORK

1 PREPARE THE BASQUAISE FILLING

2 COOK THE OMELET

1 PREPARE THE BASQUAISE FILLING

1 Peel the onion, leaving a little of the root attached, then cut it lengthwise in half. Lay each onion half flat and cut it across into thin slices.

2 Set the flat side of the chef's knife on top of each garlic clove and strike it with your fist.

3 Peel the skin from the garlic cloves with your fingers. Finely chop the cloves with the chef's knife.

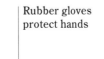
Seeds and ribs are easily cut away

5 Halve the pepper lengthwise and scrape out the seeds. Cut away the white ribs on the inside. Set each pepper half, cut-side down, on the chopping board, flatten it with the heel of your hand, and slice it lengthwise into thin strips.

4 With the small knife, cut around the red bell pepper core. Twist the core with your fingers, pull it out, and discard it.

6 Cut each chili lengthwise in half with the small knife. Cut out and discard the core. Scrape out the seeds and cut away the white ribs from each half.

! TAKE CARE !
Wear rubber gloves when preparing fresh chilis because they can burn your skin.

Rubber gloves protect hands

7 Cut each chili half into very thin strips, gather the strips together, and cut across into fine dice.

After tomatoes are blanched, skins split and slip off easily

8 Cut the cores from the tomatoes and score an "x" on the base of each one. Immerse the tomatoes in boiling water until the skins start to split, 8–15 seconds. Transfer them at once to cold water with a slotted spoon. When cool, peel, then halve the tomatoes crosswise. Squeeze out the seeds and coarsely chop each tomato half.

9 Strip the parsley leaves from the stems and pile the leaves on the chopping board. With the chef's knife, finely chop them.

10 Melt half of the butter in the frying pan, add the onion, bell and chili peppers, and cook, stirring occasionally, until the vegetables just begin to soften, 5–8 minutes.

11 Add the chopped tomatoes, garlic, and salt and pepper, and continue cooking until the mixture is thick and most of the liquid has evaporated, 5–10 minutes longer. Remove from the heat, stir in the chopped parsley, and taste the filling for seasoning.

Parsley is added after vegetables are cooked

2 COOK THE OMELET

1 Crack the eggs into a bowl, add salt and pepper, and beat with a fork until thoroughly mixed. Melt the remaining butter in the omelet pan over high heat. When it stops foaming and starts to brown, pour in the eggs. Stir briskly with the flat of the fork until the eggs start to thicken, 8–10 seconds.

2 Quickly but carefully pull the cooked egg mixture from the side of the pan to the center, then tip the pan so the uncooked egg mixture flows to the side. Continue this until the eggs are partly set, about 30 seconds.

Edge of omelet is lifted so uncooked egg runs underneath

Heavy pan is best for good omelet

3 Stir the Basquaise filling into the egg mixture and continue stirring until well mixed, 3–5 seconds. Lower the heat and leave the omelet to cook undisturbed until it is set on top and browned underneath, 2–3 minutes longer.

ANNE SAYS
"Cooking the omelet without stirring allows the bottom to brown evenly."

4 Remove the pan from the heat. Place a large plate over the top of the omelet pan and invert both the pan and plate to turn out the omelet. Slide the omelet back into the pan and brown the other side, 30–60 seconds.

Omelet is flipped to brown both sides

🍴 TO SERVE
Slide the omelet onto a warmed serving plate. Cut it into wedges and serve hot or at room temperature.

Crisp salad is colorful accompaniment to omelet

Golden omelet is filled with sweet onions and peppers

VARIATION
COUNTRY OMELET
OMELETTE PAYSANNE
This country omelet, filled with potatoes, onion, and bacon, is typical fare in French cafés.

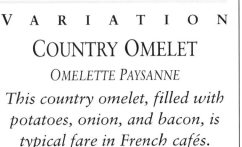

1 Omit the garlic, red bell pepper, chili peppers, and tomatoes. Slice the onion and chop the parsley as directed, reserving 1–2 small parsley sprigs for decoration.

2 Stack 1/2 lb thick-cut bacon slices on a chopping board and cut them crosswise into strips. Peel 1 lb potatoes and square off the sides. Cut the potatoes into 3/8-inch slices, stack the slices, and cut them into 3/8-inch strips. Gather the strips together into a pile and cut crosswise into cubes.

3 Heat the bacon in a large frying pan and cook over medium heat, stirring occasionally, until the fat is rendered (melted), 3–5 minutes. Discard all but 2 tbsp of the bacon fat. Stir in the onion and potatoes and continue cooking, stirring occasionally, until the onion and potatoes are tender and golden, 15–20 minutes longer. Season to taste with salt and pepper. Cook the omelet as directed, adding the potato mixture in place of the Basquaise filling.

4 To serve, cut the omelet into wedges and decorate with the reserved parsley sprigs.

SCALLOPS WITH TOMATOES, GARLIC, AND HERBS

Coquilles St. Jacques à la Provençale

🍽 SERVES 4–6   🥣 WORK TIME 20–25 MINUTES   🍲 COOKING TIME 20–25 MINUTES

EQUIPMENT

wooden spoon

chef's knife

small knife

large frying pan

slotted spoon

bowls

medium saucepan

medium sauté pan

chopping board

paper towels

INGREDIENTS

scallops

garlic cloves

fresh basil

fresh thyme

tomatoes

dry white wine

olive oil

butter

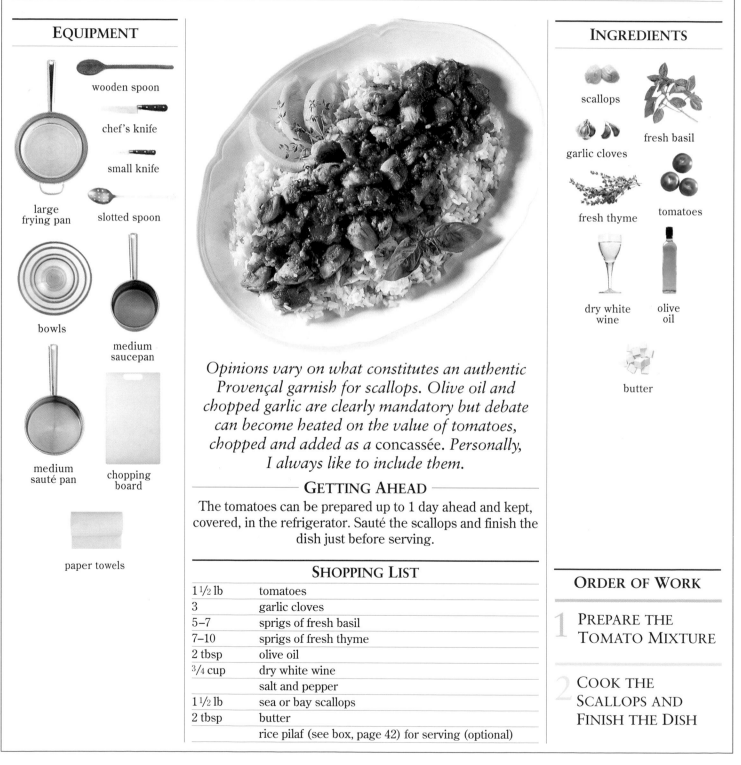

Opinions vary on what constitutes an authentic Provençal garnish for scallops. Olive oil and chopped garlic are clearly mandatory but debate can become heated on the value of tomatoes, chopped and added as a concassée. *Personally, I always like to include them.*

GETTING AHEAD

The tomatoes can be prepared up to 1 day ahead and kept, covered, in the refrigerator. Sauté the scallops and finish the dish just before serving.

SHOPPING LIST

1 1/2 lb	tomatoes
3	garlic cloves
5–7	sprigs of fresh basil
7–10	sprigs of fresh thyme
2 tbsp	olive oil
3/4 cup	dry white wine
	salt and pepper
1 1/2 lb	sea or bay scallops
2 tbsp	butter
	rice pilaf (see box, page 42) for serving (optional)

ORDER OF WORK

1 PREPARE THE TOMATO MIXTURE

2 COOK THE SCALLOPS AND FINISH THE DISH

1 PREPARE THE TOMATO MIXTURE

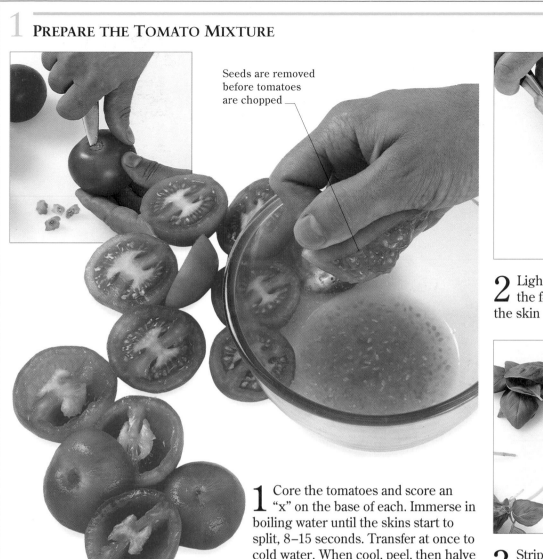

Seeds are removed before tomatoes are chopped

2 Lightly crush each garlic clove with the flat of the chef's knife. Discard the skin and finely chop the cloves.

1 Core the tomatoes and score an "x" on the base of each. Immerse in boiling water until the skins start to split, 8–15 seconds. Transfer at once to cold water. When cool, peel, then halve crosswise. Squeeze out the seeds, then coarsely chop each tomato half.

3 Strip the basil leaves from the stems and finely chop the leaves. Strip the thyme leaves from the stems.

4 Heat 1 tbsp of the oil in the sauté pan. Add the chopped garlic and cook over medium heat, stirring occasionally, until soft, 2–3 minutes.

Tomatoes and wine cook into thick sauce

Basil and thyme flavor tomatoes

5 Stir in the tomatoes, basil, thyme, wine, and salt and pepper. Simmer over medium heat, stirring occasionally, until thick enough to just fall easily from the spoon, 10–15 minutes. Taste for seasoning.

2 COOK THE SCALLOPS AND FINISH THE DISH

1 If necessary, discard the tough, crescent-shaped membrane at the side of each scallop.

2 Rinse the scallops with cold water, pat dry with paper towels, and season them with salt and pepper.

RICE PILAF

When making pilaf, the rice is first quickly fried in vegetable oil to help keep the grains separate as the rice simmers. It is then cooked in a measured amount of water so the liquid is all absorbed during cooking, leaving the rice light, tender, and flaky.

🍽 SERVES 4–6
🥣 WORK TIME 9–10 MINUTES
🍲 COOKING TIME 20 MINUTES*

* plus 10 minutes standing time

SHOPPING LIST

1	medium onion
2 tbsp	vegetable oil
1 1/2 cups	long-grain rice
3 cups	water
	salt and pepper

1 Peel and chop the onion into dice. Heat the oil in a heavy-based saucepan, add the onion, and cook, stirring, until soft, 3–5 minutes.

2 Add the rice and cook, stirring, until the oil is absorbed and the rice looks translucent, 2–3 minutes.

Stir rice in oil to keep grains separate

3 Pour the water into the saucepan, season the rice with salt and pepper, and bring to a boil.

4 Cover the pan, reduce the heat, and simmer until all the liquid is absorbed and the rice is tender, about 20 minutes. Let stand, still covered, 10 minutes, then stir with a fork.

3 Heat the butter and the remaining oil in the large frying pan. Cook the scallops until brown and slightly crisp on one side, 1 minute for bay scallops, 2 minutes for sea scallops.

4 Turn the scallops, stir in the tomato mixture, and continue cooking, 1–2 minutes.

ANNE SAYS
"The scallops should cook over high heat so the outsides become crisp, while the centers remain tender. Do not overcook them or they will be tough."

🍴 **TO SERVE**
Serve the scallops at once on a warmed platter. Accompany with rice pilaf, if you like.

Lemon wedges
are served alongside scallops

Rich Provençal sauce coats tender scallops

VARIATION
SPICED SCALLOPS
COQUILLES ST. JACQUES NANTAISE
This spicy dish comes from Nantes, in southern Brittany.

1 Omit the garlic, basil, and thyme. Brush 4 individual heatproof dishes with melted butter. Finely chop 1/2 lb tomatoes as directed. Peel a small onion and cut it lengthwise in half. Lay each half flat and slice horizontally, then vertically toward the root, leaving the slices attached. Finally, cut across into fine dice. Trim the crusts from 2 slices of white bread. Work the slices in a food processor to form crumbs.
2 Heat 1 tbsp olive oil and 1 tbsp butter in a large frying pan with 1/4 tsp curry powder and a pinch of cayenne. Cook 1 lb scallops until brown and slightly crisp, 1 minute for bay scallops, 2 minutes for sea scallops. Turn and continue cooking, 1–2 minutes. Put the scallops into the prepared heatproof dishes and cover with foil.
3 Heat the broiler. Melt 1 tbsp butter in the frying pan, then add the onion. Cook, stirring occasionally, until soft, 3–5 minutes. Add 2 tbsp brandy with the white wine and bring to a boil. Stir in the tomatoes and salt and pepper, and cook until the tomatoes are pulpy, 6–8 minutes. Taste for seasoning, then spoon the mixture over the scallops. Stir 1 tbsp melted butter into the breadcrumbs and sprinkle over the tomato mixture. Broil until the breadcrumbs are browned, 2–3 minutes. Serves 4.

ROAST SEA BASS WITH HERB BUTTER SAUCE

Loup Rôti au Beurre de Montpellier

🍽 SERVES 4　　🥣 WORK TIME 40–45 MINUTES　　♨ ROASTING TIME 30–40 MINUTES

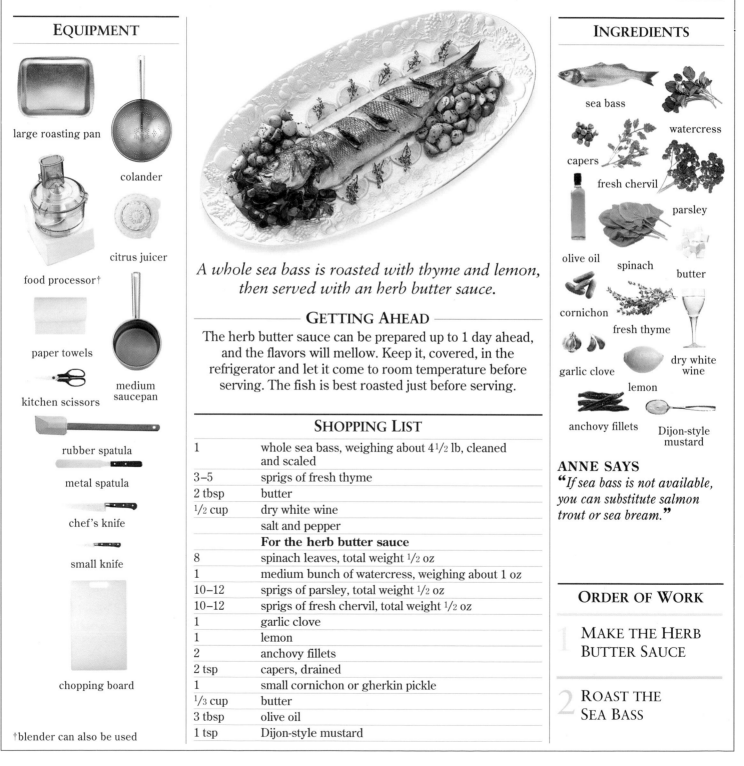

EQUIPMENT

large roasting pan

colander

food processor†

citrus juicer

paper towels

kitchen scissors

medium saucepan

rubber spatula

metal spatula

chef's knife

small knife

chopping board

†blender can also be used

A whole sea bass is roasted with thyme and lemon, then served with an herb butter sauce.

GETTING AHEAD

The herb butter sauce can be prepared up to 1 day ahead, and the flavors will mellow. Keep it, covered, in the refrigerator and let it come to room temperature before serving. The fish is best roasted just before serving.

SHOPPING LIST

1	whole sea bass, weighing about 4 1/2 lb, cleaned and scaled
3–5	sprigs of fresh thyme
2 tbsp	butter
1/2 cup	dry white wine
	salt and pepper
	For the herb butter sauce
8	spinach leaves, total weight 1/2 oz
1	medium bunch of watercress, weighing about 1 oz
10–12	sprigs of parsley, total weight 1/2 oz
10–12	sprigs of fresh chervil, total weight 1/2 oz
1	garlic clove
1	lemon
2	anchovy fillets
2 tsp	capers, drained
1	small cornichon or gherkin pickle
1/3 cup	butter
3 tbsp	olive oil
1 tsp	Dijon-style mustard

INGREDIENTS

sea bass

watercress

capers

fresh chervil

parsley

olive oil

spinach

butter

cornichon

fresh thyme

garlic clove

dry white wine

lemon

anchovy fillets

Dijon-style mustard

ANNE SAYS

"If sea bass is not available, you can substitute salmon trout or sea bream."

ORDER OF WORK

1　MAKE THE HERB BUTTER SAUCE

2　ROAST THE SEA BASS

1 MAKE THE HERB BUTTER SAUCE

Fresh young leaves are used for sauce

1 Discard any tough ribs and stems from the spinach and watercress and wash the leaves in plenty of cold water. Set aside half of the watercress for garnish.

2 Strip the parsley and chervil leaves from the stems, and add them to the spinach and watercress. Drain thoroughly.

3 Bring a medium saucepan of salted water to a boil. Add the spinach, watercress, parsley, and chervil, and simmer until tender, 1–2 minutes. Drain in the colander.

4 Rinse the greens with cold water and drain again thoroughly. Squeeze in your fist to remove excess water.

ANNE SAYS
"Rinsing the greens in cold water helps them keep their bright green color."

5 Set the flat side of the chef's knife on top of the garlic clove and strike it with your fist. Discard the skin.

6 Cut the lemon lengthwise in half. Set one half, flat-side down, on the chopping board, cut it crosswise into thin slices, and reserve for cooking the fish. Squeeze the juice from the remaining lemon half.

Strain juice to remove seeds after squeezing

8 With the blade turning, slowly pour in the olive oil. Add the lemon juice, mustard, and salt and pepper, and work again briefly. Taste for seasoning, remove, and set aside.

Mustard is added after greens have been chopped

7 In the food processor, work the garlic, anchovy fillets, capers, and cornichon until finely chopped. Add the butter, piece by piece, and work the mixture to a smooth purée. Add the greens and work until finely chopped.

2 ROAST THE SEA BASS

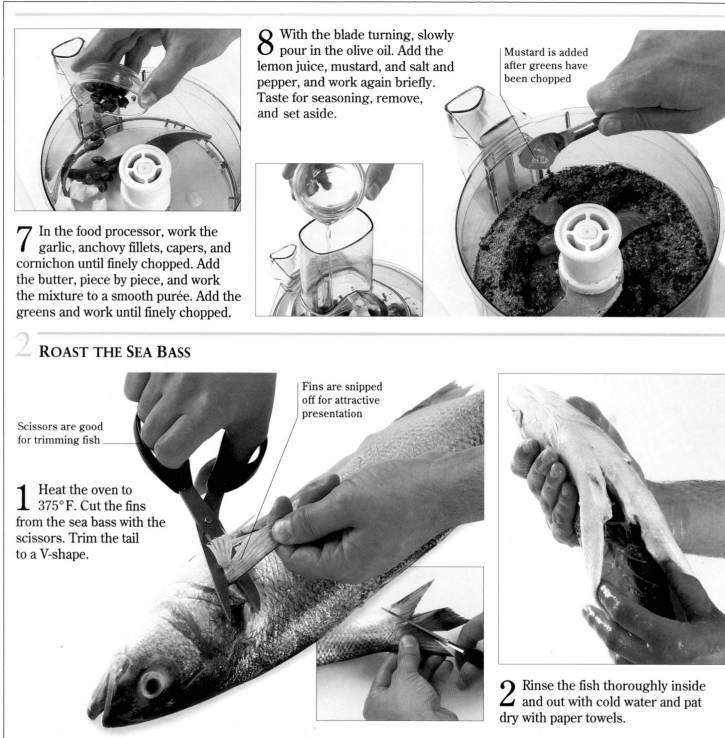

Scissors are good for trimming fish

Fins are snipped off for attractive presentation

1 Heat the oven to 375°F. Cut the fins from the sea bass with the scissors. Trim the tail to a V-shape.

2 Rinse the fish thoroughly inside and out with cold water and pat dry with paper towels.

3 With the chef's knife, slash the fish diagonally 3–4 times on each side. The slashes should be about 1/2-inch deep to allow heat to penetrate.

4 Set the sea bass in the roasting pan and tuck a sprig of thyme and a slice of lemon into each slash.

5 Dot the fish with the butter and sprinkle with white wine and salt and pepper.

Wine and butter will flavor sea bass during roasting

6 Roast the fish, basting occasionally, until it just flakes easily when tested with a fork, 30–40 minutes.

ANNE SAYS
"The fish is done when the flesh is no longer transparent in the center."

Lemon and thyme decoration echoes flavoring of roast sea bass

🍴 **TO SERVE**
Transfer the fish to a warmed platter and decorate with the reserved watercress. Serve hot or at room temperature, with the herb butter sauce handed separately.

Vibrant green herb butter sauce is served separately

LOIRE SEA BASS

LOUP ROTI, SAUCE BEURRE BLANC

Beurre blanc *originated in Brittany, near the River Loire.*

1 Omit the herb butter sauce. Roast 2 cleaned and scaled sea bass (each weighing about 2 lb) as directed, replacing the thyme sprigs with fresh tarragon, 25–30 minutes.
2 While the fish are roasting, make the sauce: peel 2 shallots and cut in half. Set flat-side down, and slice horizontally, then vertically, leaving the slices attached. Cut across to make dice.
3 In a small heavy-based pan, combine 3 tbsp each white wine vinegar and dry white wine with the shallots, then boil until reduced to about 1 tbsp, 3–5 minutes. Add 1 tbsp heavy cream, bring to a boil, and reduce to about 1 tbsp. Cut 1 cup of cold butter into small pieces. Whisk the butter into the shallots, moving the pan on and off the heat so that the butter emulsifies, thickening the sauce lightly. Do not let the base of the pan get more than hand-hot. Taste the sauce for seasoning, and keep it warm on a rack over a pan of warm water until serving.
4 Cut each fish in half and remove the head and tail. Serve with the sauce.

SWEET-SOUR DUCK WITH CHERRIES

Canard aux Cerises à l'Aigre-doux

🍴 SERVES 2–3   🥄 WORK TIME 30–35 MINUTES   🍲 COOKING TIME 1¼–1½ HOURS

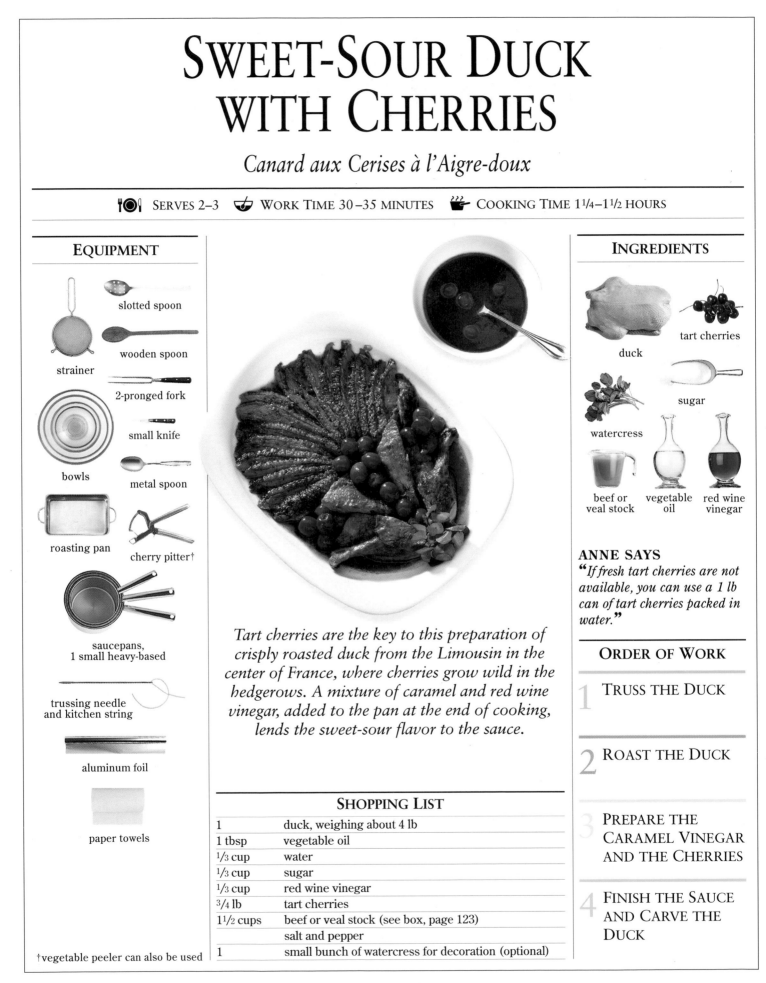

EQUIPMENT

- slotted spoon
- wooden spoon
- strainer
- 2-pronged fork
- small knife
- bowls
- metal spoon
- roasting pan
- cherry pitter†
- saucepans, 1 small heavy-based
- trussing needle and kitchen string
- aluminum foil
- paper towels

†vegetable peeler can also be used

INGREDIENTS

- duck
- tart cherries
- watercress
- sugar
- beef or veal stock
- vegetable oil
- red wine vinegar

ANNE SAYS
"*If fresh tart cherries are not available, you can use a 1 lb can of tart cherries packed in water.*"

Tart cherries are the key to this preparation of crisply roasted duck from the Limousin in the center of France, where cherries grow wild in the hedgerows. A mixture of caramel and red wine vinegar, added to the pan at the end of cooking, lends the sweet-sour flavor to the sauce.

SHOPPING LIST

1	duck, weighing about 4 lb
1 tbsp	vegetable oil
⅓ cup	water
⅓ cup	sugar
⅓ cup	red wine vinegar
¾ lb	tart cherries
1½ cups	beef or veal stock (see box, page 123)
	salt and pepper
1	small bunch of watercress for decoration (optional)

ORDER OF WORK

1 TRUSS THE DUCK

2 ROAST THE DUCK

3 PREPARE THE CARAMEL VINEGAR AND THE CHERRIES

4 FINISH THE SAUCE AND CARVE THE DUCK

1 TRUSS THE DUCK

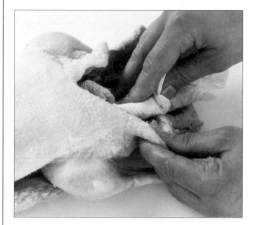

1 Wipe the inside of the duck with paper towels and season it inside and out with salt and pepper. Pull any loose bits of fat from the skin and discard them.

2 With the small knife, remove the wishbone to make the duck easier to carve.

3 Set the duck breast-side up. Push the legs back and down. Push the trussing needle into the flesh at the knee joint, through the bird and out through the other knee joint.

Hold legs of duck firmly in place while pushing through trussing needle

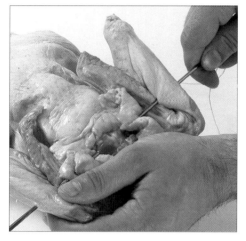

4 Turn the duck over. Pull the neck skin over the neck cavity and tuck the wing tips over it. Push the needle through one of the wings into the neck skin. Continue under the backbone of the duck to the other side. Repeat with the second wing.

Trussing string keeps duck in shape so it cooks evenly

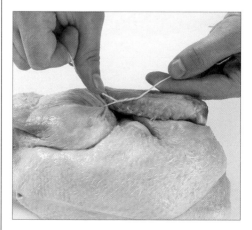

5 Turn the duck onto its side. Pull the ends of the string firmly together and tie them securely.

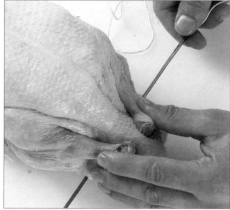

6 Turn the duck breast-side up. Tuck the tail into the cavity of the bird and fold over the top skin. Push the needle through the skin.

7 Loop the string around one of the drumsticks, under the breastbone and over the other drumstick. Tie the ends of string together.

2 ROAST THE DUCK

1 Heat the oven to 425°F. Heat the oil in the roasting pan. Set the duck on one side and roast in the oven, 15 minutes. Turn the duck onto the opposite side and roast, another 15 minutes.

Fat rendered from duck during cooking is discarded

2 Spoon the fat from the roasting pan with the metal spoon and discard it.

3 Prick the duck skin all over to release the melted fat. Lower the oven temperature to 375°F. Turn the duck onto its breast, and roast it, 15 minutes longer. Discard any more melted fat.

Use 2-pronged fork to prick duck skin

4 Finally, set the duck on its back and continue roasting until the juices from the cavity run clear, 15–20 minutes longer. Lift the duck with the 2-pronged fork and tip it to see the color of the juices. Transfer the duck to a warmed platter and cover with foil to keep warm. Meanwhile, prepare the ingredients for the sauce.

3 PREPARE THE CARAMEL VINEGAR AND THE CHERRIES

1 Put the water and sugar into the small heavy-based saucepan and heat gently until the sugar is dissolved, stirring occasionally.

2 Increase the heat and boil, without stirring, until the syrup starts to turn golden around the edge, 5–8 minutes. Lower the heat and cook to a deep golden caramel, 30–60 seconds. Remove the saucepan from the heat and let the bubbles subside.

3 Pour in the vinegar. Simmer, stirring occasionally, until the caramel is dissolved and the mixture is reduced by half, 3–5 minutes. Remove from the heat and set aside.

! TAKE CARE !
The caramel will sputter when the vinegar is added and the fumes will be strong; stand at arm's length when pouring the vinegar into the saucepan.

4 Discard any cherry stems. Pit the cherries with the pitter, or scoop out the cherry pits with the tip of a vegetable peeler. Alternatively, drain the canned cherries.

Cherry pitter removes pits easily

5 In a medium saucepan, combine the caramel vinegar and the beef or veal stock.

6 Add the cherries to the pan and simmer until they are just tender, 3–5 minutes for fresh cherries, 1–2 minutes for canned. Transfer the cherries to a bowl with the slotted spoon.

4 FINISH THE SAUCE AND CARVE THE DUCK

1 Discard any fat from the roasting pan. Add the caramel vinegar and stock mixture, and bring to a boil on top of the stove, stirring to dissolve the pan juices. Simmer until the mixture is reduced by half and the liquid is well flavored, 3–5 minutes.

2 Strain the liquid back into the saucepan. With the wooden spoon, press two-thirds of the cherries through the strainer into the liquid. Add the remaining whole cherries, bring to a boil, then add salt and pepper to taste.

Cherries are puréed to thicken sauce

Skin of duck
is crisp and
golden brown

Leg is cut
away from
body at joint

3 Place the duck breast-side up and discard the trussing string. Hold the bird steady with the 2-pronged fork and cut the skin between the legs and body, forcing the legs outward with the flat of the knife so the breast meat is revealed.

4 To remove the legs, tip the bird sideways and insert the fork into the thigh. Force the leg outward to break the joint, located well under the bird. Sever the leg, then repeat with the other leg.

6 To carve the breast, cut horizontally, just above the wing joint, through the breast meat to the bone, steadying the bird with the fork.

7 Cut long needle-shaped strips of breast meat, working the full length of the carcass, parallel to the rib cage.

ANNE SAYS
"Duck wing bones have no meat and are not normally served."

5 Halve the leg by cutting through the joint, using the line of white fat as a guide.

Use sharp
knife for
carving duck

8 Arrange the slices of breast meat in a fan shape at one end of a warmed serving platter and the leg pieces at the other. Spoon some of the cherry sauce over the duck.

🍴 TO SERVE

Decorate the duck with a bouquet of watercress, if you like, and serve at once. Serve the remaining sauce separately.

Crisp duck and tart cherries make a delicious combination

VARIATION

DUCK WITH PEARS
CANARD AUX POIRES

Pears add a mellow sweetness to this version of Sweet-Sour Duck. The pears are poached in a red wine syrup and a few are added to the sauce to thicken it.

1 Omit the cherries and beef or veal stock. Truss and roast the duck and make the caramel vinegar as directed. Combine the caramel vinegar with 1 1/2 cups red wine in a medium saucepan.

2 Meanwhile, peel 4 small pears (total weight about 1 1/4 lb) with a vegetable peeler, then cut out the flower and stem ends with a small knife. Cut each pear into quarters and scoop out the cores. At once immerse the pear quarters in the red wine mixture. Set a heatproof plate on top so the pears are completely immersed. Bring to a boil and simmer the pears until tender when tested with the tip of a knife, 8–10 minutes. Remove the pears with a slotted spoon.

3 Make the sauce, pressing 8 pear quarters through a strainer. Finish as directed, arranging a portion of leg and breast meat and 2–3 pear quarters on warmed individual plates. Spoon the sauce over the duck, and decorate with parsley sprigs, if you like.

GETTING AHEAD

The caramel vinegar and cherries can be prepared up to 12 hours ahead and kept covered. The duck is best roasted just before serving, so the skin is crisp and golden.

CORNISH HENS IN GRAPE LEAVES

Coquelets à la Vigneronne

🍽 SERVES 4   🥣 WORK TIME 45–50 MINUTES   🍲 COOKING TIME 50–60 MINUTES

EQUIPMENT

- wooden spoon
- chef's knife
- 2-pronged fork
- food processor
- ladle
- large metal spoon
- slotted spoon
- frying pans
- metal spatula
- small knife
- bowls
- kitchen string
- aluminum foil
- colander
- large casserole with lid
- paper towels
- serrated knife
- metal skewer
- strainer

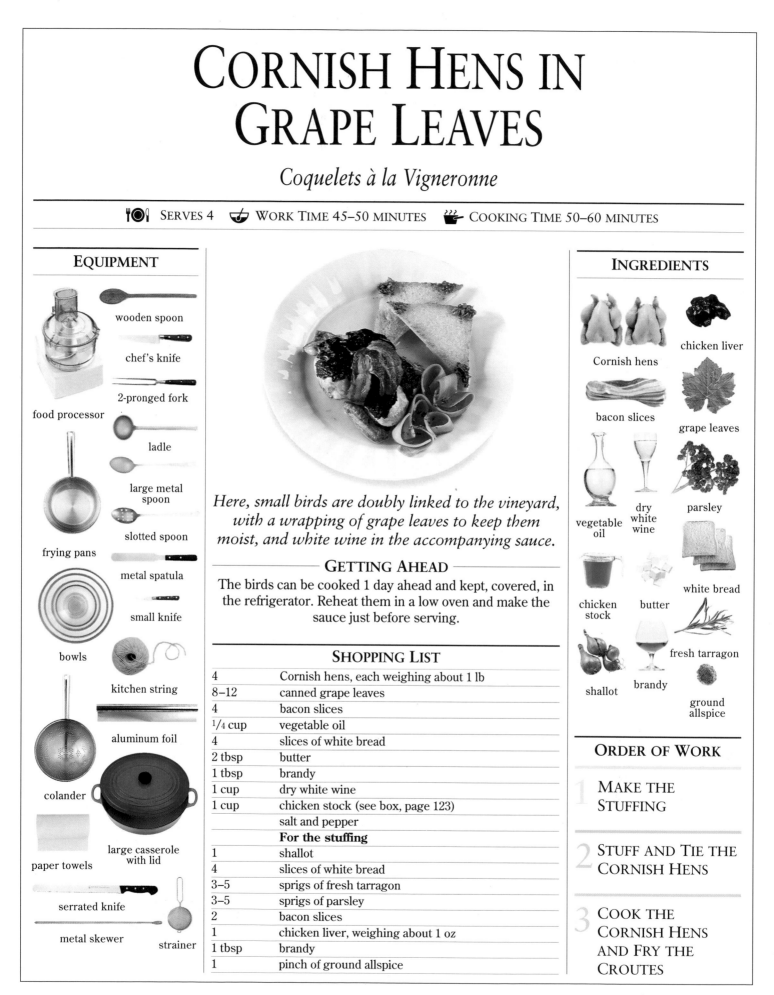

Here, small birds are doubly linked to the vineyard, with a wrapping of grape leaves to keep them moist, and white wine in the accompanying sauce.

GETTING AHEAD

The birds can be cooked 1 day ahead and kept, covered, in the refrigerator. Reheat them in a low oven and make the sauce just before serving.

SHOPPING LIST

4	Cornish hens, each weighing about 1 lb
8–12	canned grape leaves
4	bacon slices
1/4 cup	vegetable oil
4	slices of white bread
2 tbsp	butter
1 tbsp	brandy
1 cup	dry white wine
1 cup	chicken stock (see box, page 123)
	salt and pepper
For the stuffing	
1	shallot
4	slices of white bread
3–5	sprigs of fresh tarragon
3–5	sprigs of parsley
2	bacon slices
1	chicken liver, weighing about 1 oz
1 tbsp	brandy
1	pinch of ground allspice

INGREDIENTS

- Cornish hens
- chicken liver
- bacon slices
- grape leaves
- vegetable oil
- dry white wine
- parsley
- chicken stock
- butter
- white bread
- shallot
- brandy
- fresh tarragon
- ground allspice

ORDER OF WORK

1 MAKE THE STUFFING

2 STUFF AND TIE THE CORNISH HENS

3 COOK THE CORNISH HENS AND FRY THE CROUTES

MAKE THE STUFFING

Papery skin is discarded from shallot

1 Peel the shallot, leaving a little of the root attached. Cut it in half. Set each half, flat-side down, on a chopping board. Slice horizontally, then vertically, toward the root, leaving the root end uncut. Cut across into fine dice.

2 Trim and discard the crusts from the bread. Roughly tear the slices into pieces, and work them in the food processor to form crumbs. Chop the tarragon and parsley (see box, right).

3 Stack the bacon slices on the chopping board and cut them crosswise into strips about 1/4-inch wide, using the chef's knife.

Bacon is cut into thin strips

HOW TO CHOP HERBS

Parsley, dill, tarragon, rosemary, chives, thyme, and basil are herbs that are usually chopped before being added to other ingredients in a recipe. Delicate herbs such as tarragon and basil are easily bruised, so take care not to chop them too finely.

1 Strip the leaves or sprigs from the stems of the herbs, then pile the leaves or sprigs on a chopping board.

2 Cut the leaves or sprigs into small pieces with a chef's knife. Holding the tip of the blade against the board and rocking the blade back and forth, continue chopping until the herbs are coarse or fine, as you wish.

ANNE SAYS
"*Make sure that your knife is very sharp, otherwise you will bruise the herbs rather than cut them.*"

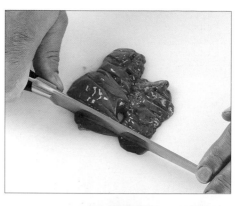

4 Trim any membrane from the chicken liver with the small knife, then coarsely chop the liver.

5 Put the bacon into a small frying pan, and cook, stirring occasionally, until crisp and the fat is rendered (melted), 3–5 minutes. With the slotted spoon, transfer the bacon to a bowl.

Chopped fresh herbs add bright color to stuffing

6 Add the shallot to the pan and cook until soft, 2–3 minutes. Add the chicken liver, sprinkle it with pepper, and cook, stirring, until brown, 1–2 minutes. Pour in the brandy and simmer, 1 minute.

7 Combine the liver mixture with the bacon. Stir in the breadcrumbs, herbs, and allspice. Season the stuffing with pepper to taste; salt may not be needed because bacon is salty.

2 STUFF AND TIE THE CORNISH HENS

Stuffing is loosely packed into cavity

Good birds have plump breast and unbroken skin with no dark patches

Herbs and bacon make tasty stuffing

1 Wipe the insides of the birds with paper towels, and season them inside and out with salt and pepper. Spoon one-quarter of the stuffing into the cavity of each bird.

3 Wrap 2 grape leaves over the breast of each Cornish hen, then top with a folded slice of bacon. Tie each bird with string like a parcel.

Wrapping of grape leaves and bacon flavors breast meat and keeps it moist

2 Rinse the grape leaves thoroughly in cold water. Drain. Place the leaves between sheets of paper towels and pat gently to dry.

ANNE SAYS
" *Two grape leaves will cover the breast of a small Cornish hen, while a larger bird requires three.*"

3 COOK THE CORNISH HENS AND FRY THE CROUTES

Use skewer to check that Cornish hens are cooked

Cornish hens are hard to brown all over but are cooked through during baking process

1 Heat the oven to 350°F. Heat half of the oil in the casserole. Add the Cornish hens and brown on all sides, 5–10 minutes. Cover the casserole and transfer it to the heated oven.

2 Bake the Cornish hens until they are tender, and the metal skewer inserted into the stuffing for 30 seconds is hot to the touch when withdrawn, 45–55 minutes. Meanwhile, make the croûtes.

Triangles make attractive shape for croûtes

3 Cut the crusts from the slices of bread, then cut each slice in half diagonally to make 2 triangles.

4 Heat the butter with the remaining oil in a large frying pan. Add the bread triangles in batches and fry on one side until golden brown, 1–2 minutes.

5 Flip the croûtes and continue frying until golden brown on the other side, 1–2 minutes longer. Remove the croûtes from the pan and drain on paper towels.

6 Transfer the Cornish hens to a platter. Discard the trussing strings, and cover the birds with foil to keep warm.

Scissors quickly remove trussing string

7 Using the large metal spoon, discard the fat from the casserole, then add the brandy and white wine.

8 Bring to a boil and simmer, stirring, until reduced by half, 5–7 minutes. Add the stock and reduce again by half, 5–7 minutes.

ANNE SAYS
"Be sure the wine is well reduced or the sauce will taste too strong."

9 Using the ladle, spoon the sauce through the strainer into a small bowl. Taste for seasoning.

⊙️ TO SERVE

Set the Cornish hens on 4 warmed individual plates and spoon over the sauce. Garnish the croûtes with chopped parsley, if you like, and set 2 beside each bird. Serve at once so the croûtes remain crisp. Leave each guest to remove the wrapping of bacon and grape leaves.

CORNISH HENS WITH BRAISED BELGIAN ENDIVE

COQUELETS AUX ENDIVES BRAISEES

Belgian endive is braised at the same time as the birds in this version of Cornish Hens in Grape Leaves. Red wine vinegar is used to deglaze the pan instead of white wine, adding a delicate tartness to the sauce.

1 Omit the grape leaves, 4 bacon slices, white wine, the brandy from the sauce, and bread croûtes.
2 Make the stuffing, and stuff, tie, and cook the Cornish hens as directed. Meanwhile, braise the Belgian endive: brush a medium baking dish with melted butter. Discard any withered outer leaves from 4 medium heads of endive (total weight about ³/₄ lb). Using a small knife, trim each endive, wipe it with a paper towel, and cut it lengthwise in half, through the core.

3 Arrange the endive halves, cut-side down, in the prepared baking dish and sprinkle with salt and pepper. Butter a piece of foil and press it down on top. Bake in the oven with the Cornish hens, turning the endive halves once or twice until they are brown and tender when pierced with the tip of a small knife, 35–40 minutes.
4 When the Cornish hens are cooked, remove and discard the trussing strings, and transfer the birds to 4 warmed individual plates. Arrange 2 endive halves beside each bird, cover with foil and keep warm while finishing the sauce. Add 2 tbsp red wine vinegar to the casserole and stir with a wooden spoon to dissolve the pan juices. Pour in 1¹/₂ cups chicken stock, add salt and pepper to taste, and simmer until the sauce is well flavored, 3–5 minutes. Taste for seasoning, strain the sauce, and spoon it around the Cornish hens.

Chopped parsley garnish enhances croûtes

Cornish hen is ideal size for individual serving

SAUTE OF CHICKEN WITH SHRIMP

Sauté de Poulet aux Crevettes

¶◉¶ SERVES 4–6   ◡ WORK TIME 25–30 MINUTES   🍲 COOKING TIME 45–55 MINUTES

EQUIPMENT

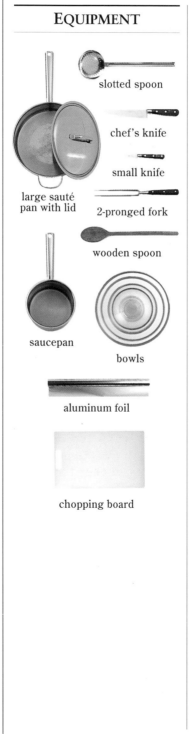

slotted spoon

chef's knife

small knife

large sauté pan with lid

2-pronged fork

wooden spoon

saucepan

bowls

aluminum foil

chopping board

The seemingly unusual combination of chicken and shellfish is traditional in Burgundy. In this recipe the chicken and shrimp are browned, then simmered in white wine and stock. A splash of marc, *a favorite Burgundian spirit, adds rich flavor.*

SHOPPING LIST

1	medium onion
2	shallots
4–6	sprigs of parsley
1/2 lb	tomatoes
2	garlic cloves
2 tbsp	butter
2 tbsp	vegetable oil
3/4 lb	raw unpeeled large shrimp
4 lb	chicken, cut into 8 pieces
3 tbsp	marc de Bourgogne
1 tbsp	tomato paste
1	bouquet garni made with 5–6 parsley stems, 2–3 sprigs of fresh thyme, and 1 bay leaf
1/4 cup	dry white wine
1/2 cup	chicken stock (see box, page 123)
	salt and pepper

INGREDIENTS

chicken pieces

marc de Bourgogne†

tomato paste

raw unpeeled large shrimp

parsley

garlic cloves

tomatoes

chicken stock

dry white wine

bouquet garni

shallots

butter

onion

vegetable oil

†brandy can also be used

ORDER OF WORK

1 PREPARE THE INGREDIENTS

2 COOK THE CHICKEN AND SHRIMP

1 PREPARE THE INGREDIENTS

1 Peel the onion, leaving a little of the root attached, and cut it lengthwise in half. Lay each half flat and slice horizontally, then vertically, leaving the root end uncut. Finally, cut across the onion to make fine dice.

Onion skins can be used for stock

2 Peel the shallots, leaving a little of the root attached. Cut them in half, and set each half, flat-side down, on the chopping board.

3 Slice each half horizontally, then vertically, toward the root, leaving the slices attached at the root end. Cut across to make fine dice.

4 Strip the parsley leaves from the stems. Pile the leaves on the chopping board and finely chop them. Peel, seed, and coarsely chop the tomatoes (see box, right).

Skin is easy to remove after crushing garlic clove

5 Set the flat side of the chef's knife on top of each garlic clove and strike it with your fist. Discard the skin and finely chop the cloves.

HOW TO PEEL, SEED, AND CHOP TOMATOES

Tomatoes are frequently peeled and seeded before chopping so they need not be strained after cooking.

1 Bring a pan of water to a boil. Using a small knife, cut out the cores from the tomatoes. Score an "x" on the base of each. Immerse in the water until the skins start to split, 8–15 seconds, depending on their ripeness. Using a slotted spoon, transfer them at once to cold water to stop them cooking.

2 When cool, peel the skin from the tomatoes with a small knife. Cut them crosswise in half and squeeze out the seeds.

3 Set each tomato half cut-side down and slice it. Give it a half turn and slice again. Chop the flesh coarsely or finely, as required.

2 COOK THE CHICKEN AND SHRIMP

1 Heat the butter and oil in the large sauté pan. Add the shrimp and sauté over high heat, stirring occasionally, until the shrimp turn pink and begin to lose their transparency, 2–3 minutes. Remove them with the slotted spoon and set aside on a plate.

Shrimp turn pink as they cook

2 Season the chicken pieces with salt and pepper and add them to the pan, skin-side down. Brown the chicken well over medium heat, about 8–10 minutes.

3 Using the 2-pronged fork, turn the chicken pieces over and brown the other side, 3–5 minutes.

4 Add the onion, shallots, and garlic, letting them fall to the bottom of the pan. Cover the pan, and cook over low heat until the vegetables are tender but not browned, 10 minutes.

5 Pour in the marc de Bourgogne and bring to a boil. Hold a lighted match to the side of the pan to set the alcohol alight. Baste the chicken until the flames subside, 20–30 seconds.

6 Add the tomatoes, tomato paste, bouquet garni, wine, stock, and salt and pepper, stir well, and bring to a boil. Cover and simmer, turning the chicken occasionally, until tender when pierced with a fork, 10–15 minutes. Transfer the chicken to a plate and cover with foil.

Stock is added after solid ingredients

Herbs in bouquet garni infuse dish with fresh aroma

7 Return the sauce to the heat, bring to a boil, and simmer until thickened slightly, 8–10 minutes.

8 Peel the shells from the shrimp, leaving the tail shells intact. Transfer the shrimp to a bowl.

9 Return the chicken and shrimp to the pan and reheat them, stirring, 1–2 minutes. Discard the bouquet garni and taste the sauce for seasoning.

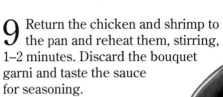

🍽 TO SERVE

Arrange the chicken pieces and shrimp on a warmed platter. Spoon the sauce over the chicken and shrimp, sprinkle with the chopped parsley, and serve at once.

Shrimp are decoratively arranged on top of chicken pieces

Chopped parsley highlights pink shrimp

V A R I A T I O N

SAUTE OF CHICKEN WITH FENNEL

SAUTE DE POULET AU FENOUIL

Fresh fennel adds a hint of anise flavor to this chicken casserole.

1 Omit the parsley, shrimp, and marc de Bourgogne. Prepare the onion, shallots, tomatoes, and garlic as directed. Slice 2 large fennel bulbs (total weight about 1½ lb): trim the stems and roots, discarding any tough outer pieces from the bulbs. Reserve a few of the fronds for garnish. Cut the bulbs in half, then set the halves, flat-side down, on the chopping board and cut them across into thin slices.

2 Brown the chicken as directed. Transfer the chicken to a plate. Add the fennel to the pan with the onions, shallots, and garlic and cook until soft, 3–5 minutes. Return the chicken to the pan, cover, and cook, 10 minutes longer. Add 2 tbsp pastis or other anise-flavored liqueur and flame the chicken. Add the tomatoes, tomato paste, wine, stock, and bouquet garni. Cook and finish the dish as directed. Decorate the chicken with the reserved fennel fronds.

GETTING AHEAD

The complete dish can be made up to 1 day ahead and kept, covered, in the refrigerator. Reheat it on top of the stove just before serving.

RABBIT WITH PROVENÇAL HERBS AND BAKED TOMATOES

Lapin aux Herbes de Provence, Tomates au Four

🍽 SERVES 4   🥣 WORK TIME 35–40 MINUTES   🍲 COOKING TIME 3–3½ HOURS

EQUIPMENT

chef's knife

boning knife

2-pronged fork

shallow non-metallic dish

cleaver

large plate

pastry brush

wooden spoon   small knife

metal spatula

aluminum foil

casserole with lid

bowls

chopping board

Herbes de Provence is a mixture of dried wild herbs – typically thyme, savory, and an anise-flavored herb such as fennel – often with a touch of sage, rosemary, and bay leaf. I enjoy marinating a rabbit or chicken in white wine with herbs while tomatoes bake slowly in the oven.

GETTING AHEAD
The rabbit stew and the tomatoes can be cooked up to 2 days ahead and kept, covered, in the refrigerator. Warm them in a 350°F oven for about 20 minutes.

SHOPPING LIST

1	rabbit, weighing about 3 lb
2	shallots
1 cup	dry white wine
¼ cup	olive oil
2 tbsp	herbes de Provence
1 tbsp	all-purpose flour
1 cup	chicken stock (see box, page 123)
4	sprigs of fresh thyme
	For the baked tomatoes
1 tbsp	olive oil, more for broiler rack
6	plum tomatoes, total weight about 1 lb
	salt and pepper

INGREDIENTS

rabbit

herbes de Provence

chicken stock

all-purpose flour

plum tomatoes

shallots

dry white wine

fresh thyme

olive oil

ANNE SAYS
"*Herbes de Provence is available in the herbs and spices section of most grocery stores.*"

ORDER OF WORK

1 CUT UP AND MARINATE THE RABBIT

2 PREPARE AND BAKE THE TOMATOES

3 COOK THE RABBIT

1 CUT UP AND MARINATE THE RABBIT

1 Using the boning knife, cut the front and hind leg sections from the rabbit, forcing the legs outward, and cutting through the joints. With the cleaver, cut the back crosswise into 4 pieces.

Use cleaver to cut through heavy backbone

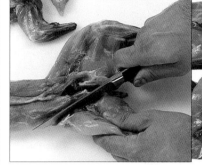

Rabbit pieces are even in size

2 Peel and chop the shallots (see box, right). Combine the white wine, half of the oil, the shallots, and herbes de Provence in the shallow non-metallic dish.

3 Add the rabbit pieces and turn until coated. Cover, and let marinate in the refrigerator, 2–3 hours. Meanwhile, prepare and bake the tomatoes.

Turn rabbit pieces once or twice during marinating

HOW TO CHOP A SHALLOT

For a standard chop, make slices that are about 1/8-inch thick. For a fine chop, make the slices as thin as possible.

1 Peel the outer, papery skin from the shallot. If necessary, separate the shallot into sections at the root and peel the sections. Set the shallot or section on a chopping board, hold it steady with your fingers, and slice horizontally toward the root, leaving the slices attached at the root end.

2 Slice vertically through the shallot, again leaving the root end uncut.

3 Cut across the shallot to make fine dice. Continue chopping, if necessary, until dice are very fine.

2 PREPARE AND BAKE THE TOMATOES

1 Heat the oven to 250°F. Brush a broiler rack with oil. Cut the cores from the tomatoes and cut each tomato lengthwise into 3 thick slices.

2 In a bowl, combine the tomatoes with the olive oil and salt and pepper. Toss until the tomatoes are coated.

3 Arrange the tomato slices on the broiler rack, and bake them in the heated oven until most of their moisture has evaporated and they are slightly shriveled, 2–2½ hours. Transfer them to a plate and cover with aluminum foil. Increase the oven temperature to 375°F.

Tomatoes should look slightly shriveled

Use metal spatula to transfer tomato slices

3 COOK THE RABBIT

2 Heat half of the remaining oil in the casserole. Add half of the rabbit pieces and cook them over medium heat until browned, about 5 minutes. Turn the pieces with the 2-pronged fork and brown the other side. Transfer them to the plate, add the remaining oil, and brown the rest of the rabbit pieces.

Browned juices in pan will make tasty sauce

1 Transfer the rabbit from the marinade to a large plate, and reserve the marinade. Season the rabbit pieces with salt and pepper.

Rabbit is flecked with herbes de Provence

3 Return all of the pieces of rabbit to the casserole and sprinkle them with the flour. Turn the rabbit pieces and cook until the flour is absorbed, 2–3 minutes.

Rabbit pieces cook in stock and rich marinade

4 Pour in the reserved marinade and the stock, and stir to mix with the rabbit. Cover, and bake, stirring occasionally, until the rabbit is very tender, 50–55 minutes. Return the tomatoes to the oven for the last 10 minutes of cooking time to heat through separately, if you like. Strip the thyme leaves from half of the stems.

⏣ TO SERVE

Arrange a rabbit leg and a piece of back meat on each of 4 warmed plates. Spoon the sauce over the rabbit and place the baked tomatoes alongside. Garnish with fresh thyme leaves and sprigs.

Herbed sauce is aromatic accompaniment for braised rabbit

Ruby tomatoes are tender and smoky in flavor from long, slow baking

CHICKEN WITH PROVENÇAL HERBS AND GARLIC POTATOES

POULET AUX HERBES DE PROVENCE, POMMES A L'AIL

Chicken replaces the rabbit in this stew, which is served with baked garlic potatoes.

1 Omit the rabbit and baked tomatoes. Chop 4 garlic cloves: lightly crush each one with the flat of a knife. Discard the skin and finely chop the cloves. Make the marinade as directed, adding half of the chopped garlic. Cut 1 chicken (weighing about 4 lb) into 8 pieces and marinate as for the rabbit.

2 While the chicken is marinating, prepare the potatoes: scrub 1½ lb new potatoes under cold running water, but do not peel. Cut each potato lengthwise into ¼-inch slices. Put them into a bowl, add the remaining garlic, 2 tbsp olive oil, and salt and pepper. Toss the potatoes until coated, then spread them on a baking sheet so each slice lies flat.

3 Heat the oven to 375°F. Brown and bake the chicken as directed for the rabbit, allowing the same cooking time. Meanwhile, bake the potatoes in the bottom third of the oven until they begin to turn golden, about 20 minutes. Turn them and continue baking until the potato slices are brown and crispy, about 20 minutes longer.

CASSOULET WITH QUICK CONFIT

🍴 SERVES 8　　🥄 WORK TIME 50–55 MINUTES*　　🍲 COOKING TIME 1³/₄–2¹/₄ HOURS

EQUIPMENT

- large flameproof casserole with lid
- colander
- plastic wrap
- paper towels
- 2-pronged fork
- chef's knife
- boning knife
- bowls, 1 non-metallic
- slotted spoon
- small knife
- large metal spoon
- wooden spoon
- heavy-duty plastic bag
- metal skewer
- saucepans
- rolling pin
- poultry shears
- chopping board

A traditional cassoulet is a slowly cooked feast of beans, confit of preserved duck or goose, and a variety of meats and sausages. Here I show you an equally delicious version, using a speedy confit, which takes a quarter of the usual time.

*plus 8–12 hours marinating time

SHOPPING LIST

¹/₂ lb	thick-cut bacon slices
1¹/₂ lb	boneless lamb shoulder
4	garlic cloves
2 lb	tomatoes
³/₄ lb	onions
³/₄ lb	country pork sausage links
³/₄ cup	dry white wine
1¹/₂ quarts	veal stock (see box, page 123) or water
	1 bouquet garni made with 5–6 parsley stems, 2–3 sprigs of fresh thyme, and 1 bay leaf
1 tbsp	tomato paste
³/₄ lb	garlic poaching sausages
3 cans	white beans, each weighing 19 oz
²/₃ cup	dried breadcrumbs
	salt and pepper
	For the quick duck confit
1	duck, weighing about 4 lb
1 tsp	black peppercorns
3–5	sprigs of fresh thyme
3	bay leaves
3 tbsp	coarse or kosher salt
1 tbsp	vegetable oil
1 tbsp	butter

INGREDIENTS

- lamb shoulder
- duck
- tomato paste
- veal stock
- white wine
- pork sausages
- bouquet garni
- garlic cloves
- poaching sausages
- onions
- thick-cut bacon slices
- vegetable oil
- butter
- tomatoes
- fresh herbs
- black peppercorns
- canned white beans
- dried breadcrumbs

ORDER OF WORK

1 **CUT UP THE DUCK**

2 **MAKE THE QUICK DUCK CONFIT**

3 **PREPARE OTHER INGREDIENTS**

4 **COOK THE MEATS, ASSEMBLE, AND BAKE THE CASSOULET**

1 CUT UP THE DUCK

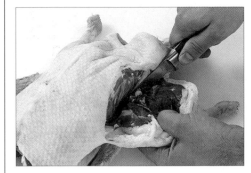

1 Trim the excess fat and skin from the duck. Using the boning knife, cut down between one leg and the body of the duck. Twist the leg sharply outward to break the joint, cut through it, and cut the whole leg from the body. Repeat with the other leg.

Boning knife should cut easily through joint

2 Cut each leg in half at the joint between the thigh and the drumstick, using the line of white fat on the underside as a guide.

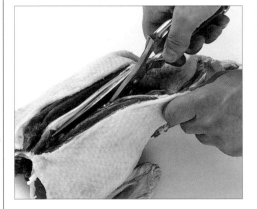

3 Slit closely along both sides of the breastbone to loosen the skin and meat from the bone. With the poultry shears or the chef's knife, cut along the breastbone to split it lengthwise in half.

4 Turn the duck over. Cut away the rib bones and backbone from the breast in one piece, leaving the breast pieces with the wing joints attached. Discard the back and rib bones.

5 Cut each breast piece diagonally in half, cutting through the bones so that a portion of the breast meat is left attached to the wing joint. Cut off any sharp bones.

ANNE SAYS
"You can ask your butcher to cut up the duck for you, but the backbone may be included. Be sure to remove it."

2 MAKE THE QUICK DUCK CONFIT

Coarse salt slowly pickles duck

1 Put the peppercorns into the plastic bag and crush them with the rolling pin. Strip the thyme leaves from the stems. Crush the bay leaves with your fingers. Combine the peppercorns, thyme, and bay leaves in a bowl.

2 Rub each piece of duck with some of the coarse salt, and put the pieces into the non-metallic bowl. Sprinkle the duck pieces with the peppercorn mixture. Cover with plastic wrap, and leave to marinate in the refrigerator, 8–12 hours.

3 Rinse the duck pieces with cold water, then wipe them with paper towels. Heat the oil and butter in the casserole. Add the duck pieces to the casserole, skin-side down, and brown them well over low heat so the fat is thoroughly melted, 20–25 minutes. Turn the pieces using the 2-pronged fork and brown the other side more quickly, about 5 minutes. Transfer to a plate and set aside.

4 Spoon all but 2 tbsp of fat from the casserole into a small bowl and discard it. Set the casserole aside for the cassoulet. Meanwhile, prepare the other ingredients.

3 PREPARE OTHER INGREDIENTS

1 Stack the bacon slices on the chopping board. Cut them crosswise into strips with the chef's knife.

2 Trim the excess fat and sinew from the lamb shoulder, then cut the meat into 2-inch cubes.

3 Set the flat side of the chef's knife on top of each garlic clove and strike it with your fist. Discard the skin and finely chop the cloves.

4 Core the tomatoes. Score an "x" on the bases. Immerse in boiling water until skins split, 8–15 seconds. Transfer to cold water. When cool, peel.

5 Cut the tomatoes crosswise in half, squeeze out the seeds, then coarsely chop each half. Peel, trim, and chop the onions (see box, below).

HOW TO CHOP AN ONION

The size of dice when chopping an onion depends on the thickness of the initial slices. For a standard size, make slices ¼-inch thick. For finely chopped onions, slice very thinly.

1 Peel the onion and trim the top; leave a little of the root attached.

2 Cut the onion lengthwise in half, through root and stem.

3 Put one half, cut-side down, on the chopping board and hold the onion steady with one hand. Using a chef's knife, make a series of horizontal cuts from the top toward the root but not through it.

4 Make a series of lengthwise vertical cuts, cutting just to the root but not through it.

ANNE SAYS
"*When slicing, tuck your fingertips under and use your knuckles to guide the blade of the knife.*"

5 Slice the onion crosswise into dice. For finely chopped onion, continue chopping until you have the fineness required.

Cut across at even intervals for neat dice

4 COOK THE MEATS, ASSEMBLE, AND BAKE THE CASSOULET

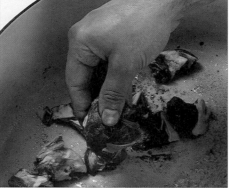

1 Heat the oven to 375°F. Heat the casserole with the reserved duck fat, add the bacon, and fry, stirring, until the fat is rendered (melted), 3–5 minutes. Transfer the bacon to a bowl with the slotted spoon.

2 Season the lamb with salt and pepper. Add the lamb in batches to the casserole and cook over high heat, stirring occasionally, until evenly browned, 3–5 minutes. With the slotted spoon, transfer the lamb to the bowl.

3 Add the country sausages to the casserole and brown them all over. Transfer the sausages to a plate. Discard all but 2 tbsp fat from the casserole. Add the onions and cook until soft, 3–5 minutes.

4 Return the lamb to the casserole with the bacon and duck confit. Add the tomatoes, white wine, and two-thirds of the stock, and stir to dissolve the pan juices.

5 Stir in the chopped garlic, bouquet garni, tomato paste, and salt and pepper. Bring to a boil on top of the stove, skimming occasionally. Cover the casserole and bake in the heated oven until the meat is almost tender, 1–1¼ hours.

ANNE SAYS
"If the meats seem dry during cooking, add more stock or water."

6 Meanwhile, put the poaching sausages into a pan with water to cover. Bring just to a boil. Simmer very gently until the skewer inserted in a sausage is warm to the touch, 20–25 minutes. Do not boil or the sausages will burst.

7 Drain the sausages and let cool until tepid. Slit the sausage skins with the small knife, then skin the sausages and cut them crosswise into ¾-inch slices.

8 Drain the beans in the colander. Rinse with cold water, and drain them again thoroughly.

9 Add both kinds of sausage and the beans to the casserole. Stir to mix, and bring just to a boil on top of the stove. The cassoulet should be very moist but not soupy. If necessary, add more stock or water. Discard the bouquet garni and taste for seasoning.

10 Sprinkle with the breadcrumbs and return to the oven. Bake, uncovered, until a golden crust forms on top and the lamb is tender, 20–25 minutes.

ANNE SAYS
"If you like, broil the casserole for 2–3 minutes to brown the breadcrumbs further."

⦿ TO SERVE
Serve the cassoulet directly from the casserole, giving each diner a combination of lamb, duck, and sausages. Sprinkle with chopped parsley, if you like.

Chopped parsley contrasts with meats and sausages

VARIATION
POOR MAN'S CASSOULET
In this version of cassoulet, the duck is omitted and pork replaces the lamb. Preparation is even less work, and the dish costs less too!

1 Omit the quick confit and lamb. Cut 1½ lb boneless pork shoulder into cubes as for the lamb. Prepare the bacon, garlic, tomatoes, and onions as directed.

2 Cook the bacon and pork as directed. Assemble and bake the cassoulet as directed, cooking both kinds of sausages and adding them with the beans. Discard the bouquet garni and taste for seasoning. Divide the cassoulet between 8 individual ovenproof dishes, sprinkle with breadcrumbs, and bake, 15–20 minutes. Sprinkle the cassoulet with chopped parsley, if you like, and serve very hot, in the dishes.

— **GETTING AHEAD** —
The cassoulet can be made up to 2 days ahead and the flavors will mellow. Keep it, covered, in the refrigerator and reheat it on top of the stove, adding a little water to thin it if necessary.

SPRING LAMB STEW

Navarin Printanier

🍽 SERVES 6   🥄 WORK TIME 45–50 MINUTES   ♨ COOKING TIME 2–2¼ HOURS

EQUIPMENT

- round casserole with lid
- medium saucepan
- bowls
- boning knife
- colander
- chef's knife
- small knife
- strainer
- wooden spoon
- slotted spoon
- vegetable peeler
- ladle
- chopping board

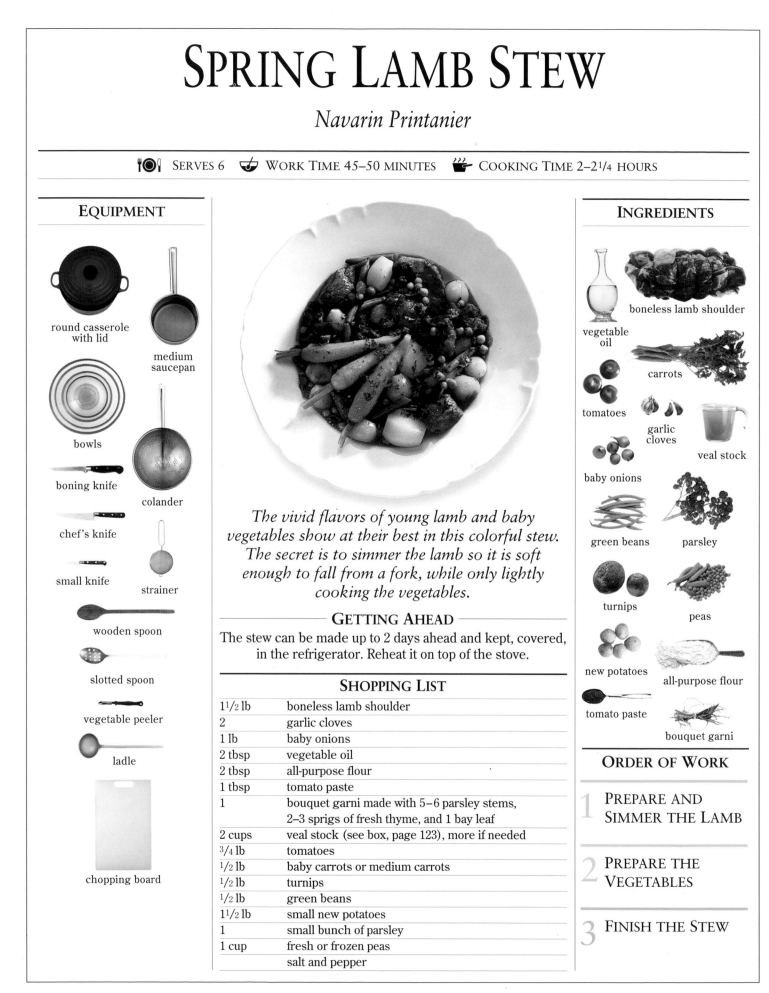

The vivid flavors of young lamb and baby vegetables show at their best in this colorful stew. The secret is to simmer the lamb so it is soft enough to fall from a fork, while only lightly cooking the vegetables.

GETTING AHEAD

The stew can be made up to 2 days ahead and kept, covered, in the refrigerator. Reheat it on top of the stove.

SHOPPING LIST

1½ lb	boneless lamb shoulder
2	garlic cloves
1 lb	baby onions
2 tbsp	vegetable oil
2 tbsp	all-purpose flour
1 tbsp	tomato paste
1	bouquet garni made with 5–6 parsley stems, 2–3 sprigs of fresh thyme, and 1 bay leaf
2 cups	veal stock (see box, page 123), more if needed
¾ lb	tomatoes
½ lb	baby carrots or medium carrots
½ lb	turnips
½ lb	green beans
1½ lb	small new potatoes
1	small bunch of parsley
1 cup	fresh or frozen peas
	salt and pepper

INGREDIENTS

- vegetable oil
- boneless lamb shoulder
- carrots
- tomatoes
- garlic cloves
- veal stock
- baby onions
- green beans
- parsley
- turnips
- peas
- new potatoes
- all-purpose flour
- tomato paste
- bouquet garni

ORDER OF WORK

1. **PREPARE AND SIMMER THE LAMB**

2. **PREPARE THE VEGETABLES**

3. **FINISH THE STEW**

1 PREPARE AND SIMMER THE LAMB

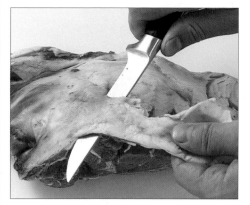

1 Using the boning knife, trim any fat and sinew from the lamb, then cut the lamb into 1–1¹/₂-inch cubes.

2 Set the flat side of the chef's knife on top of each garlic clove and strike it with your fist. Discard the skin and finely chop the cloves, moving the knife blade back and forth.

Baby onions remain firm after blanching and peeling

3 Put the baby onions into a bowl, pour over boiling water to cover, and let stand, 2 minutes. Drain the onions, then peel them, leaving a little of the root to hold them together. Heat the oil in the casserole. Add the onions and cook, stirring occasionally, until golden, 5–7 minutes. Remove with the slotted spoon and set aside.

4 Season the lamb cubes with salt and pepper, and add to the casserole, in batches if necessary. Cook over high heat, stirring occasionally, until evenly browned, 3–5 minutes. With the slotted spoon, transfer the lamb to a bowl.

5 Return all the cooked lamb to the pan, sprinkle with the flour, then stir to mix. Cook over medium heat, stirring occasionally, until the flour is browned, 2–3 minutes.

6 Let the casserole cool slightly, then stir in the tomato paste, chopped garlic, and bouquet garni. Pour in enough stock to just cover the meat, stir to mix, and bring to a boil. Cover, and simmer, 1 hour. Meanwhile, prepare the vegetables.

2 PREPARE THE VEGETABLES

1 Core the tomatoes and score an "x" on the base of each one. Immerse the tomatoes in boiling water until the skins start to split, 8–15 seconds depending on their ripeness. Using the slotted spoon, transfer the tomatoes at once to a bowl of cold water.

2 When cool, peel the skins off the tomatoes. Cut the tomatoes crosswise in half, squeeze out the seeds, then coarsely chop each tomato half.

3 If the baby carrots have green tops, trim them, leaving a little of the green, then scrape to remove the thin skin. If using medium carrots, peel them, then quarter lengthwise.

Baby carrots look neat when green tops remain

4 With the vegetable peeler, peel the turnips. Cut them into quarters or 6 or 8 wedges, depending on their size, and trim off the sharp edges with the small knife.

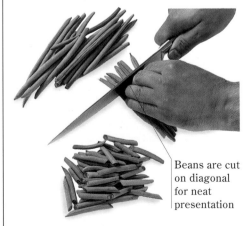

Beans are cut on diagonal for neat presentation

5 With your fingers, snap the ends off the green beans. Cut the beans into 1-inch pieces.

6 Peel the potatoes with the small knife and put them into a bowl of cold water to prevent discoloration.

7 Strip the parsley leaves from the stems, pile the leaves on the chopping board, and finely chop them.

3 FINISH THE STEW

1 With the slotted spoon, transfer the meat to a large bowl, then skim the fat from the sauce. Strain the sauce over the meat, then return the meat and sauce to the casserole. Taste the sauce for seasoning.

2 Drain the potatoes and add to the casserole with the turnips, onions, tomatoes, and carrots. Pour in stock to almost cover the meat and vegetables. Cover, and simmer, 20–25 minutes.

3 Add the peas and green beans and simmer until the lamb and vegetables are tender, 25–30 minutes longer. Taste for seasoning.

ANNE SAYS
" *The sauce should be glossy and lightly thickened. If it is thin, remove the lid when adding the peas and beans so the sauce reduces.*"

🍽 TO SERVE
Ladle the stew onto warmed plates and sprinkle with the chopped parsley.

Assortment of baby vegetables adds color to lamb stew

Lamb cubes are meltingly tender

VARIATION

LAMB RATATOUILLE
RATATOUILLE D'AGNEAU
Here, ratatouille is cooked with lamb to make a flavorful stew.

1 Omit the baby onions, tomato paste, bouquet garni, carrots, turnips, green beans, potatoes, parsley, and peas. Brown the lamb as directed, using olive oil instead of vegetable oil, then add the stock and simmer, 1¼ hours. Meanwhile, prepare the vegetables.
2 Trim 1 eggplant (weighing about 1 lb) and cut it lengthwise in half. Cut each half lengthwise into 4–5 strips, then cut across into 1-inch chunks. Put into a colander and sprinkle with salt. Let stand, 30 minutes. Meanwhile, chop 3 garlic cloves. Peel, seed, and chop 1 lb tomatoes. Core 1 green and 1 red bell pepper. Halve the peppers and scrape out the seeds and ribs. Set each half cut-side down, flatten it, and slice it lengthwise into thin strips.
3 Peel 1 large onion and cut it lengthwise in half. Lay each half flat and cut it across into thin slices. Rinse the eggplant chunks and pat dry.
4 Heat 3 tbsp olive oil in a frying pan. Add the onions and garlic and cook, stirring, until soft, 3–5 minutes. Stir in the bell pepper strips and cook, 2–3 minutes. Add the eggplant, salt and pepper, and cook, stirring often, until the vegetables are just tender, 7–10 minutes. Add the tomatoes.
5 Add the vegetables and ½ cup veal stock to the lamb. Continue cooking covered, 15 minutes, then cook uncovered until the lamb and vegetables are tender and the sauce well flavored, about 20 minutes longer. Taste for seasoning, garnish, and serve.

LEG OF LAMB WITH ROASTED GARLIC AND SHALLOTS

Gigot à l'Ail et aux Echalotes Rôtis

🍽 SERVES 8   🥣 WORK TIME 15–20 MINUTES   🍲 COOKING TIME 1¼–2 HOURS

EQUIPMENT

- shallow roasting pan
- boning knife
- small knife
- metal spoon
- 2-pronged fork
- carving knife
- metal skewer†
- aluminum foil
- wooden spoon
- slotted spoon
- chopping board

INGREDIENTS

- leg of lamb
- shallots
- garlic
- fresh thyme
- watercress
- beef stock
- dry white wine
- olive oil†

†vegetable oil can also be used

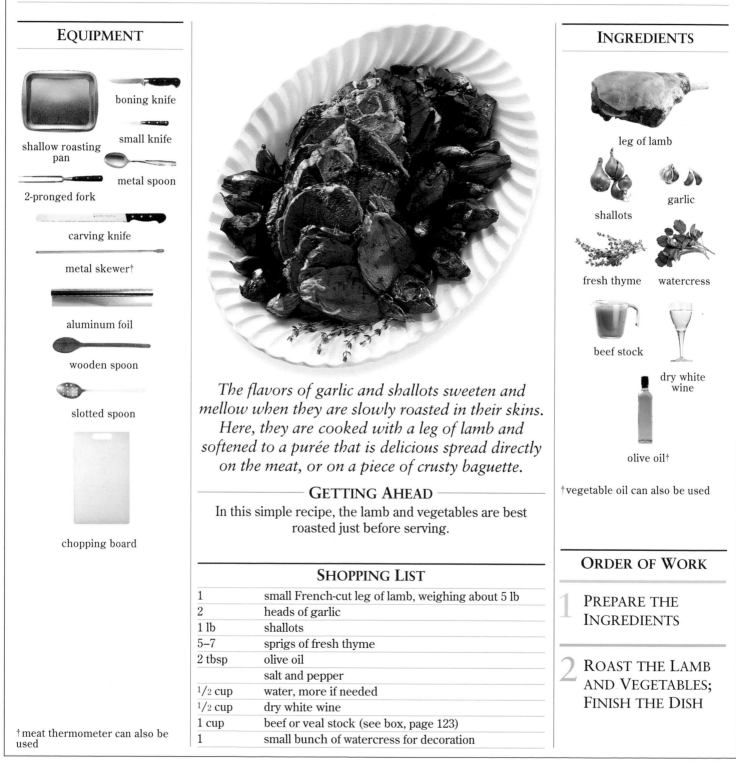

The flavors of garlic and shallots sweeten and mellow when they are slowly roasted in their skins. Here, they are cooked with a leg of lamb and softened to a purée that is delicious spread directly on the meat, or on a piece of crusty baguette.

GETTING AHEAD

In this simple recipe, the lamb and vegetables are best roasted just before serving.

SHOPPING LIST

1	small French-cut leg of lamb, weighing about 5 lb
2	heads of garlic
1 lb	shallots
5–7	sprigs of fresh thyme
2 tbsp	olive oil
	salt and pepper
½ cup	water, more if needed
½ cup	dry white wine
1 cup	beef or veal stock (see box, page 123)
1	small bunch of watercress for decoration

ORDER OF WORK

1 PREPARE THE INGREDIENTS

2 ROAST THE LAMB AND VEGETABLES; FINISH THE DISH

†meat thermometer can also be used

1 PREPARE THE INGREDIENTS

1 Heat the oven to 450°F. Using the boning knife, trim all but a thin layer of fat from the lamb.

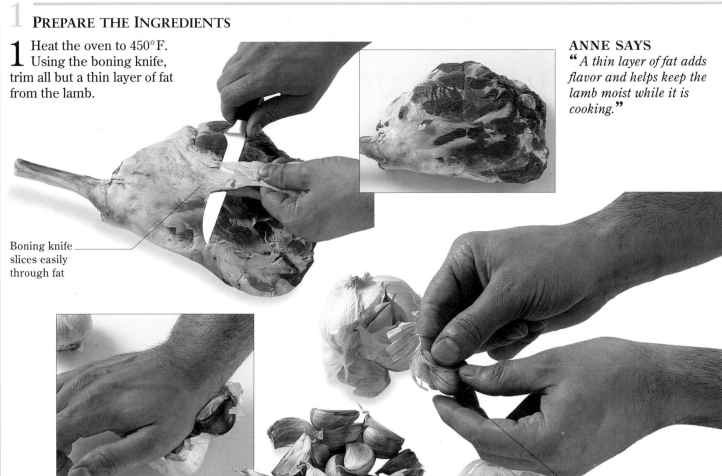

Boning knife slices easily through fat

ANNE SAYS
"A thin layer of fat adds flavor and helps keep the lamb moist while it is cooking."

Outer layer of loose papery skin is removed from garlic cloves

2 With the heel of your hand, press sharply down on the heads of garlic to loosen the cloves. Separate the cloves, and discard the root and any loose skin.

Tops of shallots are removed for neat presentation

Skin protects shallots during baking

3 With the small knife, trim the tops and roots from the shallots but do not peel them.

4 Strip the thyme leaves from half of the sprigs, and reserve the remaining sprigs for garnish.

2 ROAST THE LAMB AND VEGETABLES; FINISH THE DISH

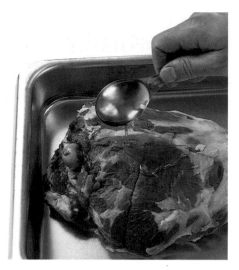

1 Put the lamb into the roasting pan and spoon over the oil. Sprinkle the lamb with the thyme leaves and salt and pepper. Roast in the heated oven until browned, 10–15 minutes.

ANNE SAYS

" Cooking at high heat forms a crust around the meat and seals in the juices."

2 Lower the oven temperature to 350°F. Add the garlic cloves and shallots to the roasting pan with the 1/2 cup water, and stir to mix with the pan juices.

3 Continue cooking the lamb, basting often, and adding a little more water if necessary, 1–1 1/4 hours for rare meat or 1 1/4–1 1/2 hours for medium done. When rare, the metal skewer inserted in the meat for 30 seconds will be cool to the touch when withdrawn, and a meat thermometer will show 125°F. When the meat is medium done, the skewer will be warm and a meat thermometer will show 140°F.

ANNE SAYS

" The garlic and shallots should be tender when pierced with the metal skewer. If necessary, continue cooking them 5–10 minutes longer."

Skewer is inserted into thickest part of leg

4 When the lamb is cooked to your taste, remove it from the pan, cover with foil, and keep warm. Remove the garlic and shallots, cover, and keep warm. Let the lamb stand 10–15 minutes before carving.

5 Meanwhile, make the gravy: discard the fat from the pan. Add the wine and bring to a boil, stirring to dissolve the pan juices. Simmer, stirring, 3–5 minutes. Stir in the stock and continue simmering until the gravy is well flavored, 2–3 minutes longer. Taste for seasoning.

Browned juices from bottom of pan are stirred into gravy

6 Carve the meat: set the lamb rounded-side up. Hold the leg by the shank and cut thin horizontal slices.

Lamb is carved into thin slices using a sawing action

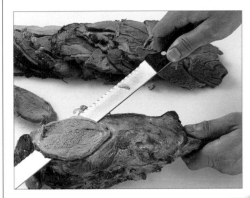

7 Turn the leg over and carve horizontal slices from the other side of the bone. Finally, carve slivers from the meat left next to the bone.

🍽 TO SERVE

Arrange the lamb, garlic, and shallots, on a warmed platter. Decorate the lamb with the reserved thyme and a watercress bouquet. Serve the gravy separately.

Roasted garlic and shallots are squeezed from their skins at the table

Fresh thyme leaves are sprinkled over lamb

V A R I A T I O N

LEG OF LAMB WITH POTATOES

GIGOT BOULANGERE

Boulangère *means baker's style, and, before every home had an oven, this dish would have been cooked by the local baker.*

1 Omit the shallots, water, white wine, and watercress. Trim the lamb as directed. Peel 4 garlic cloves. Finely chop 2 cloves and cut the other 2 into 4–5 thin slivers. Make several shallow incisions in the lamb and insert the slivers of garlic.

2 Peel 1 lb medium onions and cut them lengthwise in half. Lay each half flat and cut across into thin slices. Peel 2 lb potatoes, slice very thinly, and put them into a bowl. Strip the thyme leaves from the stems and mix with the potatoes. Cover the potatoes with a wet cloth so they do not discolor.

3 Heat 2 tbsp oil in a frying pan. Cook the onions and garlic until soft, 5–8 minutes. Stir the onion mixture into the potatoes with a pinch of nutmeg and salt and pepper. Heat the oven to 450°F.

4 Brown the lamb in a shallow baking dish as directed. Transfer to a plate. Spread the potato mixture over the bottom of the dish. Add 2 cups beef or veal stock, adding more if necessary so the potatoes are almost covered. Set the lamb on top, lower the oven heat to 350°F, and continue roasting as directed. If necessary, remove the lamb and keep warm, and continue baking the potato mixture until golden brown. Carve the lamb as directed, and serve with the potatoes and cooking juices.

STEAK AU POIVRE

EQUIPMENT

- slotted spoon
- chef's knife
- small knife
- large frying pan
- long-handled spoon
- 2-pronged fork
- vegetable peeler
- deep-fat fryer†
- bowls
- colander
- rolling pin
- shallow non-metallic dish
- heavy-duty plastic bag
- aluminum foil
- paper towels
- chopping board

†large deep saucepan can also be used

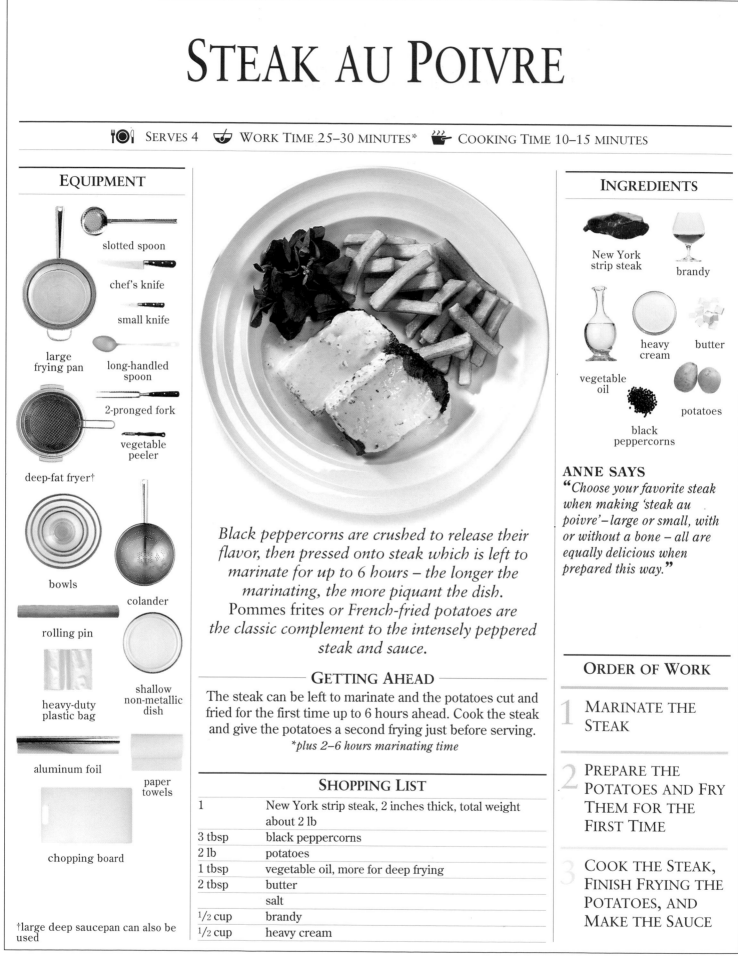

Black peppercorns are crushed to release their flavor, then pressed onto steak which is left to marinate for up to 6 hours – the longer the marinating, the more piquant the dish. Pommes frites or French-fried potatoes are the classic complement to the intensely peppered steak and sauce.

GETTING AHEAD

The steak can be left to marinate and the potatoes cut and fried for the first time up to 6 hours ahead. Cook the steak and give the potatoes a second frying just before serving.
plus 2–6 hours marinating time

SHOPPING LIST

1	New York strip steak, 2 inches thick, total weight about 2 lb
3 tbsp	black peppercorns
2 lb	potatoes
1 tbsp	vegetable oil, more for deep frying
2 tbsp	butter
	salt
1/2 cup	brandy
1/2 cup	heavy cream

INGREDIENTS

- New York strip steak
- brandy
- vegetable oil
- heavy cream
- butter
- potatoes
- black peppercorns

ANNE SAYS
"Choose your favorite steak when making 'steak au poivre' – large or small, with or without a bone – all are equally delicious when prepared this way."

ORDER OF WORK

1. **MARINATE THE STEAK**

2. **PREPARE THE POTATOES AND FRY THEM FOR THE FIRST TIME**

3. **COOK THE STEAK, FINISH FRYING THE POTATOES, AND MAKE THE SAUCE**

1 MARINATE THE STEAK

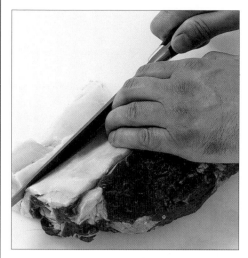

1 Trim any excess fat and sinew from the steak, leaving a thin layer of fat to flavor the meat during cooking.

2 With the small knife, slash diagonally through the fat to the beef at 1½-inch intervals.

ANNE SAYS
"This diagonal slashing cuts through the membrane that lies between the fat and the beef, and prevents the steak from buckling during cooking."

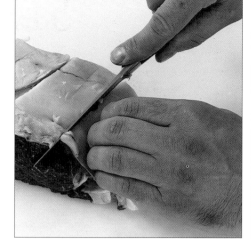

Press peppercorns firmly onto both sides of meat

Peppercorns are crushed coarsely to release flavor

4 Put the steak into the shallow dish, and, with your hands, press the crushed peppercorns onto both sides of the meat. Cover, and leave to marinate in the refrigerator, 2–6 hours. Meanwhile, prepare the potatoes.

3 Put the black peppercorns into the plastic bag and crush them with the rolling pin.

2 PREPARE THE POTATOES AND FRY THEM FOR THE FIRST TIME

Large white baking potatoes make good fries

1 Peel the potatoes. Square off the sides of each one and cut the potatoes vertically into ⅜-inch slices.

2 Stack the potato slices and cut them into ³/₈-inch sticks. Put them into a bowl of cold water to soak to remove the starch, 30 minutes.

Use knuckles to guide knife

Potatoes are dried thoroughly before frying so oil does not splatter

3 Heat the vegetable oil in the deep-fat fryer to 350°F. To test the oil temperature without a thermometer, drop in a cube of bread: it should turn golden brown in 60 seconds.

4 Remove the potato sticks from the bowl of cold water, drain them in the colander, and dry on paper towels.

6 Fry the potatoes until they are tender when pierced with the tip of a knife and are just starting to brown, 7–9 minutes. Remove the basket and let the potatoes drain over the fryer, 1–2 minutes. Transfer the potatoes to a large plate. Repeat for the remaining potatoes, frying them in 2 batches.

5 Dip the frying basket into the hot oil to prevent the potatoes from sticking to it. Lift the basket out of the oil, put in one-third of the potatoes, and carefully lower the basket into the oil.

! TAKE CARE !
Lower potatoes gradually into hot oil.

Potatoes will brown later, during second frying

3 Cook the Steak, Finish Frying the Potatoes, and Make the Sauce

1 If the potatoes were fried for the first time well in advance and the oil has cooled completely, reheat the oil in the deep-fat fryer to 375°F. To test the oil temperature, drop in a cube of bread: it should turn golden brown in about 30 seconds.

2 Heat 1 tbsp vegetable oil with the butter in the large frying pan. For a mild flavor, scrape off the pepper from the steak; for a stronger flavor, leave it on. Season the steak with salt. Put the steak into the pan, and fry it over high heat until brown, 4–6 minutes. Meanwhile, if the potatoes were fried for the first time not long in advance, and the oil is warm, reheat it in the deep-fat fryer to 375°F.

! TAKE CARE !
Do not leave hot oil unattended.

Tender steak cooks quickly

3 With the 2-pronged fork, flip the steak and continue cooking until the second side is brown, 4–6 minutes longer for rare steak, or 6–8 minutes longer for medium.

4 To test if steak is done, press it in the center with your fingertip. If spongy, it is still rare; if firm, it is well done.

5 Remove the steak from the pan and cover with foil. Pour off the fat from the pan and discard.

Lift steak out of pan with 2-pronged fork

Potatoes are
fried in batches
so they do not
crowd the pan

6 Finish frying the potatoes. Return
one-third of the potatoes to the
basket and lower it into the hot oil.
Continue frying until crisp
and golden brown,
1–2 minutes. Drain the
potatoes on paper towels.
Repeat with the remaining
potatoes.

7 Return the cooked steak to the
frying pan. Pour in the brandy and
bring it to a boil.

Steak is coated
with crisp
peppercorn crust

Brandy is
boiled before
flaming to
mellow flavor

8 Hold a lighted match to the side of
the pan to light the brandy. Baste
the steak with the pan juices until the
flames subside, 20–30 seconds.

! TAKE CARE !
*Flames can rise quite high, so stand
back and use a long-handled spoon
for basting.*

9 Transfer the steak to a carving
board, and cover to keep warm.
Add the cream to the frying pan and
simmer, stirring to dissolve the pan
juices. Taste the sauce for seasoning.

10 Trim any remaining fat from the steak, then carve the steak in diagonal slices about 1 inch thick.

🍽 TO SERVE
Divide the slices of steak among warmed individual plates and spoon the sauce on top. Sprinkle the fries lightly with salt and pile them beside the steak.
Serve at once.

V A R I A T I O N

STEAK WITH WHITE WINE AND SHALLOTS

STEAK AU VIN BLANC ET ECHALOTES

In this lighter version of Steak au Poivre, white wine, shallots, and herbs replace the brandy and cream.

1 Omit the brandy and heavy cream. Reduce the peppercorns to 1 tbsp, and marinate 4 steaks, 3/4-inch thick (total weight about 2 lb) as directed.
2 Peel 2 shallots, leaving a little of the root attached, and cut them in half. Set each half, flat-side down, on a chopping board and slice horizontally, leaving the slices attached at the root. Slice vertically, again leaving the root end uncut, then cut across the shallot to make fine dice.

3 Strip the leaves from 3–5 sprigs each of fresh tarragon, fresh thyme, and parsley. Pile the leaves on the chopping board and coarsely chop them with a chef's knife.
4 Peel the potatoes, then square off the ends and sides. Cut each one lengthwise into 1/4-inch vertical slices. Stack the slices and cut lengthwise into 1/4-inch sticks about 2 inches long; soak and dry them as directed.
5 Heat the oil in a deep-fat fryer to 350°F and fry the potatoes for the first time for 4–6 minutes as directed. Drain on paper towels.
6 Season the steaks with salt, and fry as directed. Transfer the steaks to a plate, and cover to keep warm.
7 Pour off all but 1 tbsp of fat from the frying pan, and add the shallots. Cook, stirring occasionally, until soft, 2–3 minutes. Add 1/2 cup dry white wine to the pan, stir to dissolve the pan juices, and simmer until reduced by half, 3–4 minutes. Reheat the oil in the deep-fat fryer to 375°F as directed. Add 1 cup beef or veal stock to the pan, and simmer again until reduced by half. Finish frying the potatoes as directed.
8 Take the pan from the heat, add the chopped herbs to the sauce, and taste for seasoning. Set the steaks on individual plates and serve with the sauce spooned on top. Sprinkle the fries with a little salt and pile them beside the steak.

Cream sauce mellows flavor of piquant peppercorns

PORK CHOPS WITH MUSTARD SAUCE

Côtes de Porc Dijonnaise

🍴 SERVES 4 🥣 WORK TIME 20–25 MINUTES 🍲 COOKING TIME 50–60 MINUTES

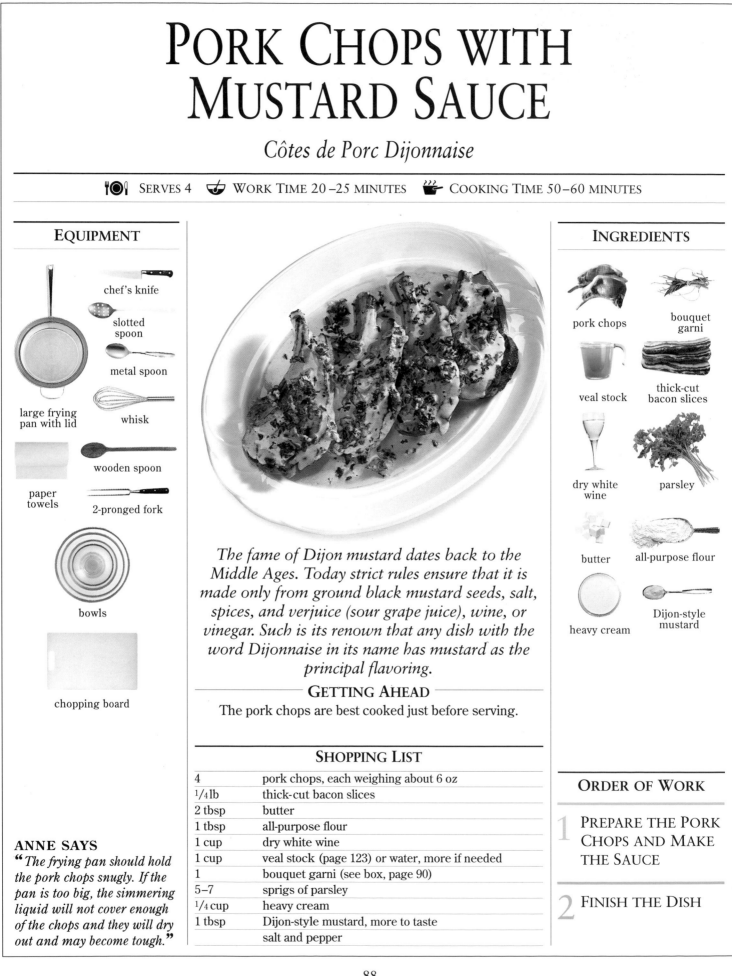

EQUIPMENT

chef's knife

slotted spoon

metal spoon

large frying pan with lid

whisk

wooden spoon

paper towels

2-pronged fork

bowls

chopping board

INGREDIENTS

pork chops

bouquet garni

veal stock

thick-cut bacon slices

dry white wine

parsley

butter

all-purpose flour

heavy cream

Dijon-style mustard

The fame of Dijon mustard dates back to the Middle Ages. Today strict rules ensure that it is made only from ground black mustard seeds, salt, spices, and verjuice (sour grape juice), wine, or vinegar. Such is its renown that any dish with the word Dijonnaise in its name has mustard as the principal flavoring.

GETTING AHEAD
The pork chops are best cooked just before serving.

SHOPPING LIST

4	pork chops, each weighing about 6 oz
1/4 lb	thick-cut bacon slices
2 tbsp	butter
1 tbsp	all-purpose flour
1 cup	dry white wine
1 cup	veal stock (page 123) or water, more if needed
1	bouquet garni (see box, page 90)
5–7	sprigs of parsley
1/4 cup	heavy cream
1 tbsp	Dijon-style mustard, more to taste
	salt and pepper

ANNE SAYS
"*The frying pan should hold the pork chops snugly. If the pan is too big, the simmering liquid will not cover enough of the chops and they will dry out and may become tough.*"

ORDER OF WORK

1 PREPARE THE PORK CHOPS AND MAKE THE SAUCE

2 FINISH THE DISH

1 PREPARE THE PORK CHOPS AND MAKE THE SAUCE

1 Trim the excess fat from the pork chops with the chef's knife, and sprinkle them with pepper.

Only lean meat is left when excess fat is removed

2 Stack the bacon slices on the chopping board and cut them crosswise into strips.

3 Heat the bacon in the frying pan, and cook, stirring occasionally, until crisp and the fat is rendered (melted), 3–5 minutes. With the slotted spoon, remove the bacon from the pan and drain on paper towels.

4 Discard all but 1 tbsp of the bacon fat. Heat the butter with the remaining bacon fat until foaming.

2-pronged fork turns chops efficiently

5 Add the pork chops to the pan and brown them well over medium heat, about 5 minutes. Turn the chops with the 2-pronged fork and brown the other side. Remove them from the pan and set aside.

Chops should be well browned

6 Remove the pan from the heat and let cool slightly, then sprinkle in the flour, and cook, stirring, 2–3 minutes.

Flour will be cooked until bubbling

7 Whisk in the white wine and veal stock or water. Add the bouquet garni and pepper, and bring to a boil.

ANNE SAYS
"Whisk constantly when adding the liquid to ensure a smooth sauce results."

8 Return the pork chops and bacon to the pan. Cover, and simmer, stirring occasionally, until the chops are tender when pierced with the 2-pronged fork, 40–50 minutes.

Chopped bacon is sprinkled all over chops

HOW TO MAKE A BOUQUET GARNI

This bundle of aromatic flavoring herbs is designed to be easily lifted from the pan and discarded at the end of cooking. To make a bouquet garni, hold together 2–3 sprigs of fresh thyme, 1 bay leaf, and 5–6 parsley stems. Wind a piece of white string around the herb stems and tie them together securely.

Always use white untreated string when cooking

Herbs infuse other ingredients with fresh aroma

9 Meanwhile, strip the parsley leaves from the stems and pile the leaves on the chopping board. With the chef's knife, finely chop them.

2 FINISH THE DISH

1 Transfer the pork chops to a plate and keep warm. Add the cream to the pan and bring just to a boil. Take the pan from the heat.

Heavy cream mellows and enriches sauce

2 Remove and discard the bouquet garni, and whisk in the mustard. Return the chops to the pan and heat gently so the flavors blend, 2–3 minutes.

! TAKE CARE !
Do not boil the sauce after adding the mustard or it will be bitter.

⏍ TO SERVE

Arrange the chops, bones pointing upward, on a warmed platter. Taste the sauce for seasoning, whisking in more mustard if you like. Spoon the sauce over the chops, then sprinkle with the parsley.

Parsley and bacon add bright color to mustard sauce

VARIATION

VEAL CHOPS WITH MUSTARD SAUCE AND BABY ONIONS

CÔTES DE VEAU DIJONNAISE AUX PETITS OIGNONS

Veal chops take the place of the pork, while sweet baby onions replace the smoky flavor of the bacon.

1 Omit the pork chops, bacon, and parsley. Prepare 4 veal chops (each weighing about 1/2 lb) as for the pork chops. Put 1 lb baby onions into a bowl, pour over boiling water to cover, and let stand, 2 minutes. Drain the baby onions, then peel them, leaving a little of the root to hold them together.

2 Heat 1 tbsp vegetable oil in a frying pan, add the baby onions, and cook, stirring, until golden brown, 5–7 minutes. Remove the onions with a slotted spoon. Heat 2 tbsp butter in the pan and brown the veal chops as directed for the pork chops. Pour in the white wine and veal stock or water, and add the bouquet garni. Cover, then simmer the veal chops, 20 minutes. Add the onions and continue cooking until the chops and onions are tender, 20–30 minutes longer. Finish the sauce as directed.

ZUCCHINI TIAN

Tian de Courgettes

🍽 SERVES 6   🥣 WORK TIME 30–35 MINUTES   🍲 COOKING TIME 20–30 MINUTES

EQUIPMENT

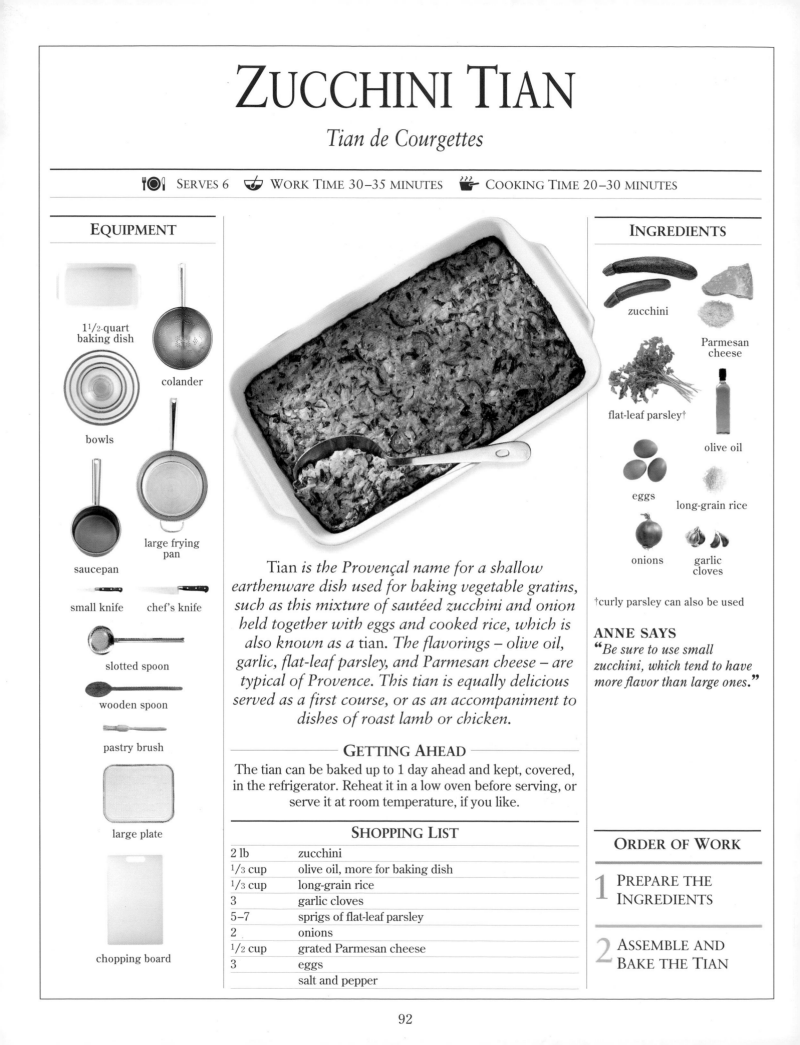

1¹/₂-quart baking dish

colander

bowls

large frying pan

saucepan

small knife   chef's knife

slotted spoon

wooden spoon

pastry brush

large plate

chopping board

INGREDIENTS

zucchini

Parmesan cheese

flat-leaf parsley†

olive oil

eggs

long-grain rice

onions   garlic cloves

†curly parsley can also be used

ANNE SAYS
"Be sure to use small zucchini, which tend to have more flavor than large ones."

Tian *is the Provençal name for a shallow earthenware dish used for baking vegetable gratins, such as this mixture of sautéed zucchini and onion held together with eggs and cooked rice, which is also known as a* tian. *The flavorings – olive oil, garlic, flat-leaf parsley, and Parmesan cheese – are typical of Provence. This tian is equally delicious served as a first course, or as an accompaniment to dishes of roast lamb or chicken.*

GETTING AHEAD
The tian can be baked up to 1 day ahead and kept, covered, in the refrigerator. Reheat it in a low oven before serving, or serve it at room temperature, if you like.

SHOPPING LIST

2 lb	zucchini
¹/₃ cup	olive oil, more for baking dish
¹/₃ cup	long-grain rice
3	garlic cloves
5–7	sprigs of flat-leaf parsley
2	onions
¹/₂ cup	grated Parmesan cheese
3	eggs
	salt and pepper

ORDER OF WORK

1 **PREPARE THE INGREDIENTS**

2 **ASSEMBLE AND BAKE THE TIAN**

1 PREPARE THE INGREDIENTS

1 Trim the zucchini, then cut them crosswise into 1/4-inch slices with the chef's knife.

2 Heat one-third of the oil in the large frying pan. Add the zucchini and salt and pepper, and cook over medium heat, stirring occasionally, until tender and brown, 10–15 minutes.

3 Transfer the zucchini from the pan to the large plate. Let cool. Meanwhile, cook the rice.

Zucchini should be nicely browned

Spread zucchini over plate to cool

HOW TO SLICE AN ONION

Onions are often sliced for soups and stews, as well as for sautéing. The root end is left on for slicing, to help hold the onion together.

1 Using a chef's knife, cut the onion lengthwise in half through the root and stem ends.

2 Lay each half, cut-side down, on a chopping board, and cut across into thin or thick slices, as required.

Cut onion into slices of even thickness

4 Bring a saucepan of salted water to a boil, add the rice, and bring back to a boil. Simmer until just tender, stirring occasionally, 10–12 minutes.

5 Drain the rice in the colander, rinse with cold water, and drain again thoroughly. Let the rice cool, 8–10 minutes, then stir with a fork to separate the grains.

6 Set the flat side of the chef's knife on top of each garlic clove and strike it with your fist. Discard the skin and finely chop the cloves.

7 Strip the parsley leaves from the stems and pile the leaves on the chopping board. Using the chef's knife, finely chop them.

8 Peel the onions with the small knife, leaving a little of the root attached. Halve and thinly slice the onions (see box, page 93). Heat half of the remaining oil in the frying pan, add the onions and garlic and cook, stirring occasionally, until soft, 3–5 minutes.

2 ASSEMBLE AND BAKE THE TIAN

2 In a large bowl, combine the chopped zucchini, onion mixture, parsley, rice, and Parmesan cheese. Stir to mix, then taste for seasoning.

Parmesan adds robust flavor

1 Heat the oven to 350° F. Brush the baking dish with oil. Coarsely chop the cooled zucchini.

3 Crack the eggs into a bowl and beat to mix. Stir them into the vegetable mixture with the wooden spoon.

4 Spread the mixture over the baking dish and sprinkle with the remaining oil. Bake the tian in the heated oven until set, 10–15 minutes. Increase the oven temperature to 400°F and bake until brown, 10–15 minutes longer.

Edges of tian are crisp, while the center is creamy

🍽 **TO SERVE**

Serve the tian directly from the baking dish, hot or at room temperature.

Tian is served as accompaniment to roast meats and poultry

V A R I A T I O N

SPINACH AND MUSHROOM GRATIN
TIAN D'EPINARDS ET CHAMPIGNONS

Spinach and mushrooms are a tasty alternative to zucchini.

1 Omit the zucchini, rice, and parsley. Trim the crusts from 2 slices of white bread. Work the bread slices in a food processor to form fine crumbs. Chop the onions and garlic as directed.
2 Discard the tough ribs and stems from 2 lb spinach, then wash the leaves. Bring a large saucepan of salted water to a boil. Add the spinach, and simmer until tender, 1–2 minutes. Drain the spinach, rinse with cold water, and drain again. Squeeze the spinach in your fist to remove excess water, then chop coarsely. Wipe 3/4 lb mushrooms, trim the stems, then thinly slice the caps.
3 Heat 2 tbsp olive oil in a large frying pan and cook the onions and garlic as directed. Add the mushrooms to the pan and sauté until tender, about 5 minutes. Add the spinach and salt and pepper and continue cooking, stirring occasionally, until all the liquid has evaporated, about 5 minutes longer. Let the vegetable mixture cool, then stir in the Parmesan cheese. Taste for seasoning. Prepare a baking dish as directed.
4 Beat the eggs, then stir them into the vegetable mixture. Spoon into the prepared baking dish and sprinkle with the breadcrumbs and 2 tbsp olive oil. Bake as directed.

CREAMY SCALLOPED POTATOES

Gratin Dauphinois

🍽 SERVES 6–8   🥣 WORK TIME 30–40 MINUTES   🍲 BAKING TIME 20–25 MINUTES

EQUIPMENT

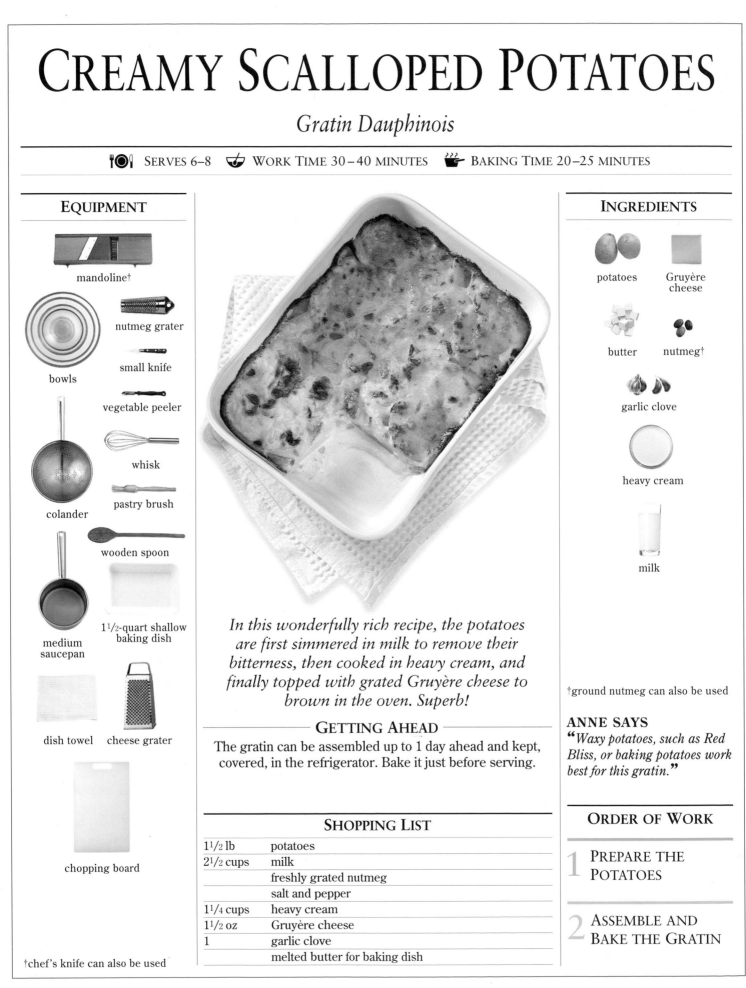

mandoline†

nutmeg grater

small knife

bowls

vegetable peeler

whisk

pastry brush

colander

wooden spoon

medium saucepan

1½-quart shallow baking dish

dish towel   cheese grater

chopping board

†chef's knife can also be used

INGREDIENTS

potatoes   Gruyère cheese

butter   nutmeg†

garlic clove

heavy cream

milk

†ground nutmeg can also be used

ANNE SAYS

"Waxy potatoes, such as Red Bliss, or baking potatoes work best for this gratin."

In this wonderfully rich recipe, the potatoes are first simmered in milk to remove their bitterness, then cooked in heavy cream, and finally topped with grated Gruyère cheese to brown in the oven. Superb!

GETTING AHEAD

The gratin can be assembled up to 1 day ahead and kept, covered, in the refrigerator. Bake it just before serving.

SHOPPING LIST

1½ lb	potatoes
2½ cups	milk
	freshly grated nutmeg
	salt and pepper
1¼ cups	heavy cream
1½ oz	Gruyère cheese
1	garlic clove
	melted butter for baking dish

ORDER OF WORK

1 PREPARE THE POTATOES

2 ASSEMBLE AND BAKE THE GRATIN

96

1 PREPARE THE POTATOES

1 Peel the potatoes. With the mandoline, cut the potatoes crosswise into 1/8-inch slices. Alternatively, with the chef's knife, cut a thin slice from one side of each potato so the potatoes sit flat on the chopping board, and cut them into 1/8-inch slices. Cover the slices with the wet dish towel so they do not discolor.

! TAKE CARE !
Do not soak the potatoes in water. This removes the starch that will give the gratin its creamy consistency.

Keep fingertips away from blade of mandoline

Potatoes are thinly sliced so they are tender after baking

2 Bring the milk to a boil in the medium saucepan. Season it with a little grated nutmeg, and salt and pepper.

! TAKE CARE !
Stir the milk occasionally with a whisk so that it does not burn.

3 Add the potatoes and cook, stirring occasionally, until the potatoes are just tender, 10–15 minutes.

Freshly grated nutmeg is more aromatic than ground

4 Drain the potatoes in the colander. Discard the milk, or save it for another use such as soup, if you like.

2 ASSEMBLE AND BAKE THE GRATIN

1 Return the potatoes to the saucepan and pour in the cream. Bring to a boil and simmer, stirring occasionally, until the potatoes are very tender, 10–15 minutes. Taste for seasoning.

ANNE SAYS
"After cooking, the cream should be just lightly thickened with starch from the potatoes."

Cream will be simmered gently so it does not evaporate

Potatoes should not break up during cooking

2 Using the coarsest grid of the cheese grater, grate the cheese; set aside. Heat the oven to 375°F.

3 Peel the garlic clove, cut it in half, and use the cut side to rub the bottom and sides of the baking dish.

5 Arrange the potatoes and cream in the prepared baking dish, then sprinkle with the grated cheese.

4 Brush the bottom and sides of the baking dish with melted butter, using the pastry brush.

Grated cheese is sprinkled evenly over potatoes

6 Bake the gratin in the heated oven until golden brown, 20–25 minutes. Test with the small knife; the blade should feel hot when withdrawn.

🍴 **TO SERVE**
Serve the scalloped potatoes hot, directly from the baking dish.

Scalloped potatoes are an excellent accompaniment to broiled and roast meats

Twice-cooked potatoes are meltingly tender

VARIATION
GRATIN OF ROOT VEGETABLES
GRATIN DE RACINES D'HIVER

Root vegetables replace half of the potatoes in this version of Gratin Dauphinois. I have chosen carrots, but any root vegetable, such as celery root or turnips, will do. The carrot slices can be arranged in alternate rows with the potatoes.

1 Peel and trim ³⁄₄ lb carrots. Thinly slice the carrots with a mandoline or chef's knife. Bring 1¹⁄₄ cups milk to a boil, and season with a little grated nutmeg, and salt and pepper. Add the carrots and simmer until they are almost tender, 15–20 minutes.
2 Meanwhile, peel and slice ³⁄₄ lb potatoes, and simmer them in another 1¹⁄₄ cups milk as directed. Prepare 6 individual baking dishes as directed for the large baking dish.
3 Drain the carrots and potatoes in a colander. Simmer them together in the cream, and finish the gratin as directed. Serves 6.

CHERRY CLAFOUTIS

Clafoutis aux Cerises

🍽 SERVES 6–8   🥣 WORK TIME 20–25 MINUTES   ♨ BAKING TIME 30–35 MINUTES

EQUIPMENT

whisk

2-quart shallow baking dish

ladle

pastry brush

strainer

cherry pitter†

small strainer

bowls

metal spoon

chopping board

INGREDIENTS

cherries

confectioners' sugar

granulated sugar

egg yolks

heavy cream

all-purpose flour

kirsch

eggs

butter

milk

In this dessert from the Limousin in central France, cherries are baked in an egg batter that puffs up and turns golden. Tart cherries give the most flavor; I like to remove the pits, though this is not traditional. Whipped cream is the best accompaniment.

GETTING AHEAD

The clafoutis is best freshly baked and served warm, but it can also be cooked up to 6 hours ahead and served at room temperature.

ANNE SAYS
"If fresh cherries are not available, you can use two 1-lb cans of cherries packed in water."

ORDER OF WORK

1 PREPARE THE CHERRIES AND MAKE THE BATTER

2 ASSEMBLE THE CLAFOUTIS

SHOPPING LIST

	butter for baking dish
1/2 cup	granulated sugar, more for baking dish
1 1/4 lb	cherries
1/3 cup	all-purpose flour
	salt
2/3 cup	milk
1/3 cup	heavy cream
4	eggs
2	egg yolks
3 tbsp	kirsch
2 tbsp	confectioners' sugar

†vegetable peeler can also be used

100

1 PREPARE THE CHERRIES AND MAKE THE BATTER

1 Brush the baking dish with melted butter. Sprinkle some granulated sugar into the dish. Turn the dish around and shake it to coat the bottom and side evenly.

2 Turn the dish upside down and tap the base with your knuckles to remove any excess sugar.

3 Pit the fresh cherries (see box, below). Alternatively, drain the canned cherries. Spread the cherries in an even layer over the bottom of the prepared baking dish.

4 Sift the flour and a pinch of salt into a medium bowl and make a well in the center with your fingers.

HOW TO PIT CHERRIES

Choose firm cherries with a shiny skin; avoid any with a dry stem.

Use tip of vegetable peeler to work pit from cherry

To pit with a cherry pitter: push the pit through the fruit, leaving a hollow. Pitting allows more of the juice to be released when the cherries are cooked.

To pit with a vegetable peeler: insert the tip in the stem end, rotate around the pit, and scoop it out. The result is neater than if a cherry pitter is used, and more of the juices will be retained.

Eggs and sugar are added to flour mixture at same time

5 Pour the milk and cream into the well and stir with a whisk, gradually drawing in the flour to make a smooth paste.

6 Add the eggs, egg yolks, and granulated sugar, and continue whisking to make a smooth batter.

ANNE SAYS
"*There is no need to whisk the batter vigorously.*"

Additional egg yolks add richness to clafoutis

2 ASSEMBLE THE CLAFOUTIS

Batter is easy to pour with ladle

Batter partly covers cherries

1 Heat the oven to 350°F. Just before baking, ladle the batter over the cherries, then spoon over the kirsch.

2 Bake the clafoutis in the heated oven until puffed up and beginning to brown, 30–35 minutes.

ANNE SAYS
"*When cooked, the clafoutis will pull away from the side of the baking dish.*"

3 Just before serving, sprinkle the clafoutis with the confectioners' sugar, using the small strainer.

🍴 TO SERVE

Serve the clafoutis warm or at room temperature, with whipped cream if you like.

V A R I A T I O N

PLUM CLAFOUTIS

CLAFOUTIS AUX PRUNES

Clafoutis with cherries is a dessert of early summer. In autumn and winter, other fresh or dried fruits are used instead, such as any type of small plum.

1 Omit the cherries. Prepare the baking dish and make the batter as directed.

2 Cut 1¹/₄ lb small plums in half around the pit. Using both hands, give a quick, sharp twist to each half to loosen it from the pit. Scoop out the pit with the tip of a small knife and discard it.

3 Arrange the plums, cut-side up, in the bottom of the prepared baking dish. Assemble, bake, and decorate the clafoutis as directed.

Juicy cherries stud sweet rich batter

Confectioners' sugar decorates top of cherry clafoutis

APRICOT AND HAZELNUT ICE CREAM

Glace Auxerroise

🍴 SERVES 6   🥄 WORK TIME 35–40 MINUTES*   ❄ FREEZING TIME AT LEAST 4 HOURS**

EQUIPMENT

chef's knife

whisk

food processor†

ice-cream scoop

strainer

bowls

small knife

ice-cream maker

dish towel

plastic wrap

small jar with lid

rubber spatula

wooden spoon

saucepans, 1 heavy-based with lid

†blender can also be used

Vanilla ice cream is transformed by hazelnuts and dried apricots in this Burgundian recipe. A hazelnut liqueur, such as Frangelico, adds sparkle.

GETTING AHEAD

The ice cream can be made up to 2 weeks ahead and kept, tightly covered, in the freezer. If it has been frozen more than 12 hours, let it soften for about 30 minutes in the refrigerator before serving.

*plus up to 2 days soaking time
**freezing time varies according to the ice-cream maker you use

SHOPPING LIST

2/3 cup	dried apricot halves
3/4 cup	hazelnut liqueur
1 cup	hazelnuts
For the vanilla ice cream	
2 1/2 cups	milk
1	vanilla bean
2/3 cup	sugar
8	egg yolks
2 tbsp	cornstarch
1 cup	heavy cream

INGREDIENTS

dried apricot halves

milk

sugar

cornstarch

hazelnuts

vanilla bean†

heavy cream

egg yolks

hazelnut liqueur‡

†1 tsp vanilla extract can also be used

‡apricot brandy can also be used

ORDER OF WORK

1 PREPARE THE APRICOTS AND HAZELNUTS

2 MAKE THE VANILLA CUSTARD

3 FREEZE THE ICE CREAM

1 PREPARE THE APRICOTS AND HAZELNUTS

1 Put the apricots into a bowl and pour over enough boiling water to cover them. Let soak, 10–15 minutes.

2 Drain the apricots and put them into the small jar. Pour over the hazelnut liqueur and cover tightly. Let soak, at least 2 hours, and up to 2 days.

Hazelnut liqueur is reserved to serve with ice cream

Apricots will have more flavor the longer they macerate

3 Strain the apricots, reserving the liqueur. Purée the apricots in a food processor and set aside.

4 Toast and skin the hazelnuts (see box, right). With the chef's knife, coarsely chop the hazelnuts. Reserve half of the nuts for serving.

ANNE SAYS

"If you are making the ice cream well ahead, store the reserved hazelnuts and liqueur in covered containers."

HOW TO TOAST AND SKIN NUTS

Toasting nuts intensifies their flavor and adds crunch to their texture. It also loosens the skin from nuts such as hazelnuts for easy removal.

Hazelnut skins will come off easily after toasting

1 Heat the oven to 350°F. Spread the nuts on a baking sheet and toast until lightly browned, stirring occasionally, 12–15 minutes.

2 While the nuts are still hot, rub them in a dish towel to remove the skins, then let cool.

2 MAKE THE VANILLA CUSTARD

1 Pour the milk into the heavy-based saucepan. Cut the vanilla bean lengthwise, if using. Add to the pan. Bring the milk just to a boil. Remove from the heat. Cover, and let stand in a warm place, 10–15 minutes.

2 Set aside one-quarter of the milk. Add the sugar to the remaining hot milk and stir with the wooden spoon until dissolved.

3 Beat the egg yolks with the cornstarch in a medium bowl. Add the sweetened hot milk and whisk just until the mixture is smooth.

4 Pour the custard back into the saucepan and cook over medium heat, stirring constantly with the wooden spoon, until it comes just to a boil and thickens enough to coat the back of the spoon. Your finger will leave a clear trail across the spoon.

5 Remove the pan from the heat, stir in the reserved milk, then strain the custard into a bowl. Stir in the vanilla extract, if using. Cover tightly with plastic wrap to prevent a skin forming on the surface of the custard and let cool.

ANNE SAYS
"The vanilla bean can be rinsed and dried to use again."

Custard is strained to remove vanilla bean and any bits of cooked egg yolk

3 FREEZE THE ICE CREAM

1 If the vanilla custard has formed a skin, whisk to dissolve it. Pour the custard into the ice-cream maker and freeze until slushy, following the manufacturer's directions. Meanwhile, chill 2 medium bowls in the freezer.

2 Pour the cream into one of the chilled bowls and whip until soft peaks form.

ANNE SAYS
"Cream thickens faster when whipped in a chilled bowl."

3 Add half of the hazelnuts and the apricot purée to the slushy vanilla ice cream and stir until mixed.

Use rubber spatula to stir ice cream

PRUNE AND ARMAGNAC ICE CREAM
GLACE GASCONNE

A combination of two Gascon favorites, prunes and Armagnac, flavors this ice cream – a fine end to any festive meal.

4 Add the whipped cream, stir lightly, and continue freezing in the ice-cream maker until firm. Transfer the ice cream to the second chilled bowl. Cover tightly and store in the freezer.

Hazelnuts give crunchy finish to ice cream

1 Omit the apricots, hazelnut liqueur, and hazelnuts. Put ³/₄ cup pitted prunes into a small bowl. Pour over ³/₄ cup Armagnac and let the prunes soak as directed for the apricots. Strain the prunes, reserving the liqueur. Purée the prunes.

2 Make and chill the vanilla custard as directed. Make and freeze the ice cream as directed, substituting the prunes and Armagnac for the apricots and hazelnut liqueur. Serve the ice cream with the reserved liqueur as directed, topped with more pitted prunes, if you like.

🍴 **TO SERVE**
Scoop the ice cream into chilled individual glasses and spoon over the reserved hazelnut liqueur. Top with the reserved hazelnuts, and serve at once.

Tall sundae glasses are ideal for serving ice cream

GOLDEN RICE PUDDING WITH PEACHES AND RED WINE

Terrinée et Chicolle

🍽 SERVES 4–6   🥣 WORK TIME 15–20 MINUTES*   🍲 COOKING TIME 4 HOURS

EQUIPMENT

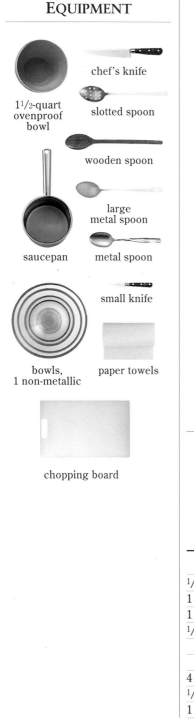

chef's knife

1¹/₂-quart ovenproof bowl

slotted spoon

wooden spoon

large metal spoon

saucepan

metal spoon

small knife

bowls, 1 non-metallic

paper towels

chopping board

The long cooking for this rice pudding results in a creamy dessert hidden beneath a sweet golden crust. In summer, I like to serve it just warm, accompanied by chilled peaches macerated in red wine.

GETTING AHEAD

Both the rice pudding and peaches can be prepared 1 day ahead and kept, covered, in the refrigerator. Let the rice come to room temperature, or warm it in a low oven before serving.

* plus at least 2 hours macerating and 1 hour standing time

SHOPPING LIST

¹/₃ cup	short-grain rice
1 quart	milk, more if needed
1	2-inch piece of cinnamon stick
¹/₄ cup	sugar
	salt
	For the chicolle
4	ripe peaches
¹/₃ cup	sugar, more if needed
1 cup	dry red wine, more if needed

INGREDIENTS

peaches

short-grain rice

milk

dry red wine

sugar

cinnamon stick

ANNE SAYS

"Short-grain rice contains more starch than long or medium-grain rice and absorbs more milk, making the pudding richer."

ORDER OF WORK

1 **MACERATE THE PEACHES IN RED WINE**

2 **MAKE THE RICE PUDDING**

1 MACERATE THE PEACHES IN RED WINE

Blanched peaches retain their shape

1 Peel and pit the peaches: bring a saucepan of water to a boil. Immerse the peaches in the water, 10 seconds, then transfer them to a bowl of cold water.

Peaches are cooled in cold water so they do not cook

ANNE SAYS
"If the peaches are very ripe, you may not need to put them into boiling water before peeling."

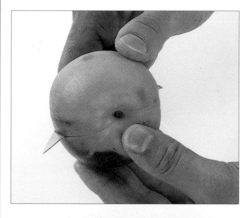

2 Using the small knife, cut each peach in half, using the indentation on one side as a guide.

3 With both hands, give a sharp twist to each peach half to loosen it from the pit. If the peaches cling, loosen the flesh from the pit with a knife.

5 Carefully peel the skin from each of the peach halves and discard it.

Skin is removed before peaches are macerated in red wine

Peach skin peels away easily

4 Lift or scoop out the pit from the center of each peach half and discard it.

6 Cut each peach half into 2 wedges and put them into the non-metallic bowl.

Peaches may need more or less sugar depending on their sweetness

7 Sprinkle the peaches with sugar, then pour over the red wine, adding more if necessary to cover the fruit completely.

8 Set a plate on top to weigh down the peaches. Leave to macerate in the refrigerator, at least 2 hours and up to 24 hours.

2 MAKE THE RICE PUDDING

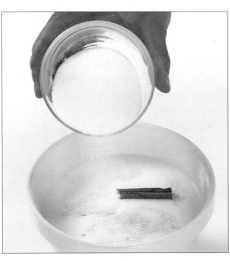

2 Wipe the side of the bowl clean with a damp paper towel. Transfer the bowl to the heated oven and bake. Stir the mixture gently every 30 minutes by slipping the metal spoon down the side of the bowl and stirring from the bottom, until a golden crust forms, 4 hours. The pudding will be soupy throughout cooking.

! TAKE CARE !
At the end of cooking, a golden crust will form. Try not to break the crust.

1 Heat the oven to 300°F. In the ovenproof bowl, combine the rice, milk, cinnamon stick, sugar, and a pinch of salt. Stir with the wooden spoon until well mixed.

Cinnamon stick flavors rice pudding during long cooking

3 Remove the pudding from the oven. Carefully slip the spoon down the side of the bowl, and stir the mixture from the bottom. Let the pudding stand to completely absorb the milk, 1 hour.

ANNE SAYS
"The pudding will be soupy until it cools."

⑩ TO SERVE
Remove and discard the cinnamon stick from the rice pudding. Divide the pudding among individual bowls, then spoon over the peaches with some of the red wine syrup.

V A R I A T I O N

RICE PUDDING WITH DRIED FRUIT COMPOTE

TERRINEE AU CONFIT DE FRUITS SECS

A quickly cooked compote of dried fruit – half fruit salad, half preserve – adds a contrast of texture and flavor to creamy rice pudding.

1 Omit the peaches, 1/3 cup sugar, and the red wine. Prepare the rice pudding as directed. Meanwhile, prepare the dried fruit compote.

2 Cut 1/2 cup dried figs into eighths and 1/2 cup dried apricot halves across into 4 slices each. With a vegetable peeler, peel the zest from 1 lemon half.

3 Put the lemon zest into a small saucepan with 7 tbsp sugar and 1 whole clove. Add 3/4 cup water and heat, stirring occasionally, until the sugar dissolves. Bring to a boil, add the figs, and simmer until softened, about 5 minutes.

4 Add the apricots and 2 tbsp golden raisins and continue simmering until the fruit is puffed up and tender, about 5 minutes more.

5 Remove the pan from the heat, stir in 2 tbsp brandy, and let stand until all the liquid is absorbed, 5–10 minutes. Remove and discard the whole clove. Serve the compote warm or hot with the rice pudding.

Red wine syrup is refreshing accompaniment to creamy rice pudding

Peach wedges are richly flavored with wine

SNOW EGGS

Oeufs à la Neige

🍴 SERVES 8   🥣 WORK TIME 35–40 MINUTES   🍲 COOKING TIME 45–50 MINUTES

EQUIPMENT

slotted spoon

wooden spoon

small frying pan

whisk

small knife

large metal bowl

paper towels

rubber spatula

bowls

medium heavy-based saucepan with lid

large wide pan

strainer

dessert spoons

plastic wrap

baking sheet

INGREDIENTS

sugar

sliced almonds

vanilla bean†

milk

egg yolks

egg whites

cornstarch

†1 tsp vanilla extract can also be used

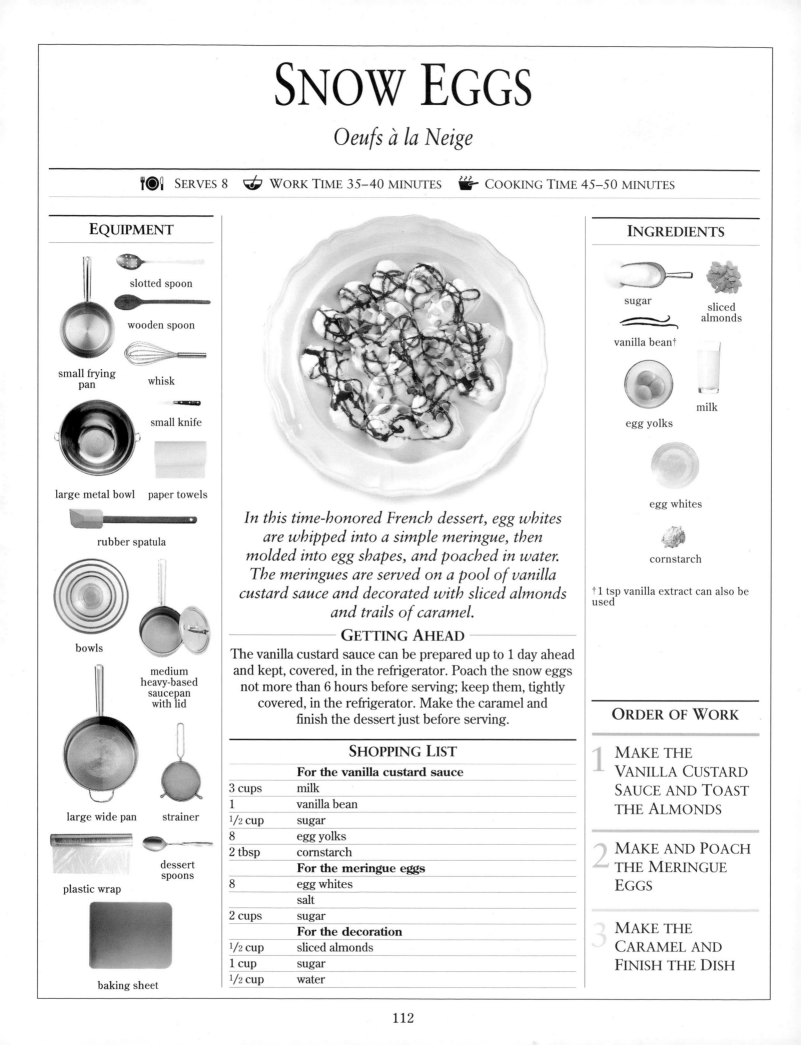

In this time-honored French dessert, egg whites are whipped into a simple meringue, then molded into egg shapes, and poached in water. The meringues are served on a pool of vanilla custard sauce and decorated with sliced almonds and trails of caramel.

GETTING AHEAD

The vanilla custard sauce can be prepared up to 1 day ahead and kept, covered, in the refrigerator. Poach the snow eggs not more than 6 hours before serving; keep them, tightly covered, in the refrigerator. Make the caramel and finish the dessert just before serving.

SHOPPING LIST

For the vanilla custard sauce	
3 cups	milk
1	vanilla bean
1/2 cup	sugar
8	egg yolks
2 tbsp	cornstarch
For the meringue eggs	
8	egg whites
	salt
2 cups	sugar
For the decoration	
1/2 cup	sliced almonds
1 cup	sugar
1/2 cup	water

ORDER OF WORK

1 MAKE THE VANILLA CUSTARD SAUCE AND TOAST THE ALMONDS

2 MAKE AND POACH THE MERINGUE EGGS

3 MAKE THE CARAMEL AND FINISH THE DISH

1 MAKE THE VANILLA CUSTARD SAUCE AND TOAST THE ALMONDS

1 Pour the milk into the saucepan. Cut the vanilla bean lengthwise, if using, and add to the milk. Bring the milk just to a boil, then remove the pan from the heat. Cover, and let stand in a warm place, 10–15 minutes.

2 Set aside one-quarter of the milk. Add the sugar to the remaining hot milk and stir until dissolved.

Sugar dissolves quickly in hot milk

3 Beat the egg yolks with the cornstarch in a medium bowl. Add the sweetened hot milk and whisk just until the mixture is smooth.

4 Pour the custard back into the saucepan and cook over medium heat, stirring constantly, until it comes just to a boil and is thick enough to coat the back of the spoon; the custard will curdle if boiled further.

Finger leaves clear trail across spoon

5 Remove the pan from the heat, stir in the reserved milk, then strain the custard into a bowl. Rinse the vanilla bean, dry, and store to use again. Stir in the vanilla extract, if using. Cover tightly with plastic wrap to prevent a skin from forming on the surface of the custard, and let cool. Finally, chill the custard sauce.

Reserved milk adjusts consistency of custard

6 Heat the oven to 350°F. Spread the almonds on the baking sheet and toast in the heated oven until lightly browned, stirring occasionally so they color evenly, 10–12 minutes. Set the almonds aside.

2 MAKE AND POACH THE MERINGUE EGGS

Egg whites are whisked while sugar is added

Egg whites are shaped into neat ovals

1 Put the egg whites into the metal bowl with a pinch of salt and whisk until stiff. Sprinkle in 5–6 tbsp of the sugar, and continue whisking until glossy to make a light meringue, about 30 seconds.

2 Using the rubber spatula, fold the remaining sugar into the meringue mixture gradually and thoroughly, 1–2 minutes, or until the meringue forms long peaks when the spatula is lifted from the bowl.

3 Bring a large wide pan of water to a simmer. Dip a dessert spoon into the water, and scoop out a large spoonful of meringue. Use a second spoon to shape the meringue into a neat oval, turning the spoons one against the other.

5 Lift the meringue eggs out of the water with the slotted spoon and drain on paper towels. Shape and cook the remaining meringue in the same way.

ANNE SAYS
"The meringue eggs will deflate slightly as they cool."

4 Drop the meringue egg into the simmering water. Quickly continue shaping 6–7 more eggs, dipping the spoons into the water so they do not stick. Poach the eggs until firm and puffed, 5–7 minutes.

Meringues are drained on paper towels to remove excess water

3 MAKE THE CARAMEL AND FINISH THE DISH

1 Pour the chilled custard sauce into a wide shallow serving dish. Using the slotted spoon, arrange the meringue eggs over the custard.

2 Make the caramel: put the sugar and water into a small frying pan and heat gently until the sugar is dissolved, stirring occasionally. Bring the sugar syrup to a boil, and boil without stirring until the syrup starts to turn golden around the edge, 8–10 minutes.

3 Lower the heat and continue cooking until the caramel is a deep golden brown, swirling it in the pan once or twice so it colors evenly. Remove the pan from the heat and immediately plunge the base into a bowl of cold water to stop the caramel cooking.

! TAKE CARE !
Do not overcook the caramel because it burns easily.

4 Dry the base of the pan, then delicately drizzle the caramel over the meringue eggs in a freeform pattern. Alternatively, drizzle the caramel with a spoon.

¶Ⓞ¶ TO SERVE
Sprinkle the snow eggs with the toasted almonds and serve immediately.

Toasted almonds make a crunchy contrast to light snow eggs and creamy sauce

Caramel gives attractive finish

VARIATION

CHOCOLATE SNOW EGGS

OEUFS A LA NEIGE AU CHOCOLAT
Here, a chocolate custard sauce accompanies the meringue eggs, which are topped with trails of melted chocolate.

1 Omit the caramel, sliced almonds, and vanilla bean or vanilla extract. Cut 10 oz semisweet chocolate into large chunks. Chop them with a chef's knife, or in a food processor using the pulse button.
2 Make the custard sauce using two-thirds of the chopped chocolate instead of the vanilla bean or vanilla extract. Heat the milk gently, stirring, until melted and smooth. Do not let the milk come to a boil. Continue making the custard sauce as directed.
3 Make and poach 18 meringue eggs as directed. Heat the reserved chopped chocolate in a bowl set in a saucepan of hot water, stirring occasionally, until just melted.
4 Spoon the chocolate custard into 6 shallow individual bowls and divide the snow eggs among them. With a spoon, drizzle the melted chocolate over the snow eggs. Serves 6.

RUSTIC APPLE TART

Tarte aux Pommes Ménagère

🍴 SERVES 6–8   🥣 WORK TIME 40–45 MINUTES*   ♨ BAKING TIME 30–40 MINUTES

EQUIPMENT

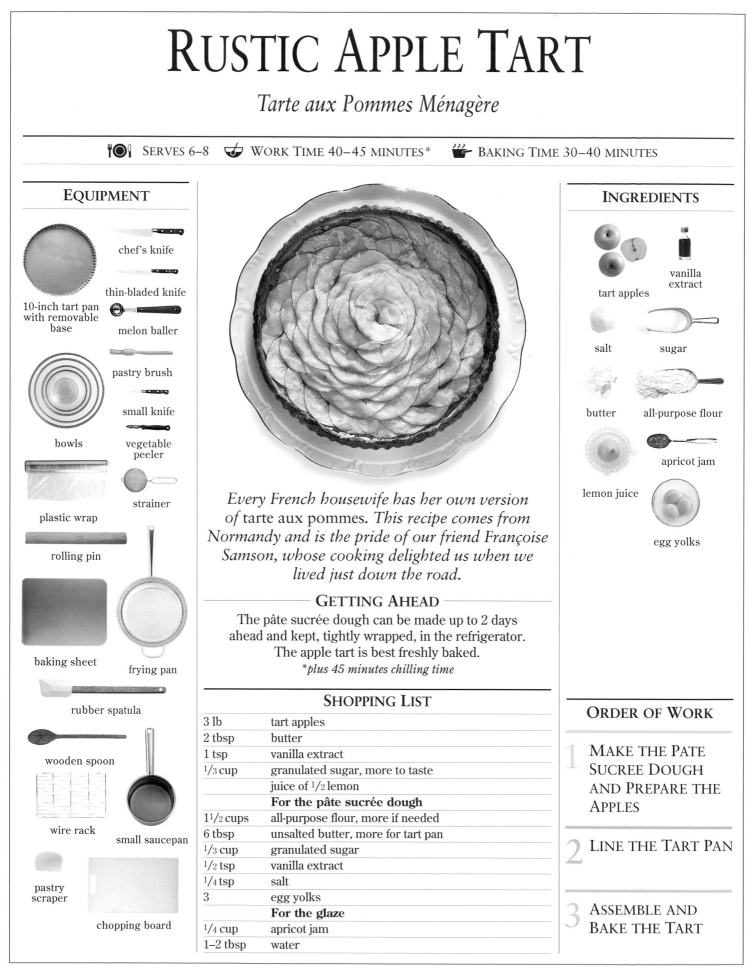

- chef's knife
- thin-bladed knife
- melon baller
- pastry brush
- small knife
- vegetable peeler
- 10-inch tart pan with removable base
- bowls
- strainer
- plastic wrap
- rolling pin
- baking sheet
- frying pan
- rubber spatula
- wooden spoon
- wire rack
- small saucepan
- pastry scraper
- chopping board

INGREDIENTS

- tart apples
- vanilla extract
- salt
- sugar
- butter
- all-purpose flour
- lemon juice
- apricot jam
- egg yolks

Every French housewife has her own version of tarte aux pommes. *This recipe comes from Normandy and is the pride of our friend Françoise Samson, whose cooking delighted us when we lived just down the road.*

GETTING AHEAD

The pâte sucrée dough can be made up to 2 days ahead and kept, tightly wrapped, in the refrigerator. The apple tart is best freshly baked.

plus 45 minutes chilling time

SHOPPING LIST

3 lb	tart apples
2 tbsp	butter
1 tsp	vanilla extract
1/3 cup	granulated sugar, more to taste
	juice of 1/2 lemon
	For the pâte sucrée dough
1 1/2 cups	all-purpose flour, more if needed
6 tbsp	unsalted butter, more for tart pan
1/3 cup	granulated sugar
1/2 tsp	vanilla extract
1/4 tsp	salt
3	egg yolks
	For the glaze
1/4 cup	apricot jam
1–2 tbsp	water

ORDER OF WORK

1   MAKE THE PATE SUCREE DOUGH AND PREPARE THE APPLES

2   LINE THE TART PAN

3   ASSEMBLE AND BAKE THE TART

1 MAKE THE PATE SUCREE DOUGH AND PREPARE THE APPLES

Turn knife blade around stem of apple to remove it

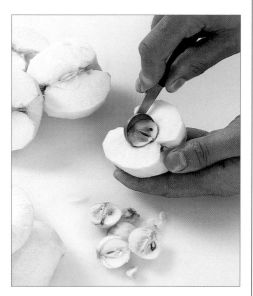

1 Make and chill the pâte sucrée dough (see box, page 118). Make the apple compote: using the vegetable peeler, peel two-thirds of the apples. Cut out the flower and stem ends of the apples with the small knife.

2 Using the chef's knife, cut each apple in half, then scoop out the cores with the melon baller.

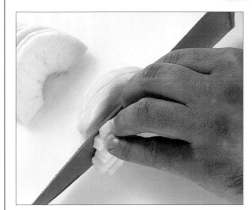

3 Set 1 apple half, flat-side down, on the chopping board. Cut it crosswise into 1/4-inch slices. Stack the slices and cut them into 1/4-inch strips.

Apple dice cook gently in butter

4 Gather the strips together into a pile and cut crosswise into dice. Repeat with the remaining apples.

5 Melt the butter in the frying pan. Add the apples, vanilla extract, and all but 2 tbsp of the sugar. Cook over medium-high heat, stirring often, until the apples are very soft and almost a purée, 10–15 minutes. Taste the apples, adding more sugar if needed. Let cool.

HOW TO MAKE PATE SUCREE DOUGH

The favorite French sweet pastry is pâte sucrée. The high proportion of sugar and eggs yolks gives the dough a crumbly character, much like a biscuit.

1 Sift the flour onto the work surface and make a well in the center. Pound the butter with a rolling pin to soften it.

2 Put the sugar, softened butter, vanilla extract, salt, and egg yolks into the well.

Well in flour is large enough for ingredients to be mixed easily

3 With your fingertips, work the ingredients in the well until thoroughly mixed.

4 Draw in the flour with the pastry scraper, then work the flour into the other ingredients with your fingers until coarse crumbs form.

5 With your fingers, press the crumbs firmly together to form a ball of dough. If the dough is sticky, work in a little more flour. Lightly flour the work surface.

6 Blend the dough by pushing it away from you with the heel of your hand, then gathering it up, until it is very smooth and peels away from the work surface, 1–2 minutes.

7 Shape the dough into a ball, wrap it tightly in plastic wrap, and chill until firm, about 30 minutes.

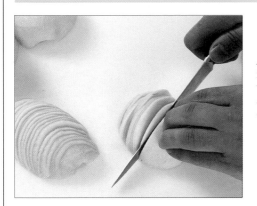

Apples are cut
into thin slices
to arrange in
attractive pattern
on tart

Lemon juice
prevents apple
slices from
discoloring

6 Peel and core the remaining apples. Set each apple half, flat-side down, on the chopping board. With the thin-bladed knife, cut the apple halves crosswise into thin slices.

7 Transfer the apple slices to a medium bowl, sprinkle with the lemon juice, and toss to coat completely.

2 LINE THE TART PAN

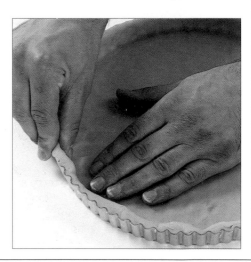

1 Brush the tart pan with melted butter. Lightly flour the work surface and roll out the chilled dough into a 12-inch round.

2 Wrap the dough around the rolling pin, then drape it over the pan. Gently lift the edge of the dough with one hand and press it well into the bottom of the pan with the other hand, pressing to seal any cracks. Overlap the dough slightly inside the rim of the pan so that extra dough is left at the edge of the shell.

Excess dough
will be cut away
with rolling pin

Rolling pin
gives clean
edge to dough

3 Roll the rolling pin over the top of the pan, pressing down to cut off the excess dough.

4 Press the dough evenly up the side, from the bottom, to increase the height of the shell. Chill until firm, about 15 minutes. Heat the oven to 400°F. Put the baking sheet into the oven to heat.

ANNE SAYS
"A deep shell leaves plenty of room for filling."

3 ASSEMBLE AND BAKE THE TART

Apple slices are arranged from outside edge to center of tart

1 Spoon the cooled apple compote over the bottom of the pastry shell. Arrange the apple slices over the compote in overlapping concentric circles. Sprinkle with the remaining sugar.

2 Bake the tart on the baking sheet in the heated oven, until the rim of the pastry begins to turn golden, 15–20 minutes. Lower the oven temperature to 350°F and continue baking the tart until the apple slices are tender and the rim of the pastry is golden brown, 15–20 minutes longer. Let the tart cool slightly on the wire rack, then set the tart pan on a bowl to loosen and remove the side.

ANNE SAYS
"*The edges of the apple slices should brown to form an attractive pattern. If necessary, broil the tart 2–3 minutes to brown it.*"

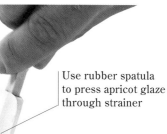

Use rubber spatula to press apricot glaze through strainer

Glaze is strained to ensure that it is smooth

3 Let the tart cool a little longer, then slide it from the pan base onto a serving platter.

! TAKE CARE !
Do not remove the pan base too soon or the pastry may crack.

4 Meanwhile, make the glaze: in a small saucepan, heat the apricot jam with the water, stirring until melted. Work the jam glaze through a strainer. Return the glaze to the pan and melt again over low heat.

5 Brush the apples and the pastry rim with the apricot glaze.

Brush gently so that apple slices are not dislodged

Apricot glaze gives tart brilliant shine

🍽 TO SERVE

Serve warm or at room temperature with crème fraîche or vanilla ice cream, if you like.

Layer of sliced apples conceals filling of sweet apple compote

V A R I A T I O N

APPLE TARTLETS

TARTELETTES AUX POMMES

When baked in tartlet molds, family-style apple tart becomes an elegant dessert. This recipe makes 6 tartlets.

1 Make the pâte sucrée dough and prepare the apples as directed in the main recipe.

2 Brush six 4-inch tartlet molds with melted butter. Lightly flour the work surface and roll out the chilled dough to an $1/8$-inch thickness. Group the tartlet molds together, with their edges nearly touching. Drape the dough over the molds and line them as directed. With your fingers, press the dough well into the bottom of each mold and against the side to form a neat shell. Chill until firm, about 15 minutes.

3 Heat the oven to 400°F. Put a baking sheet in the oven to heat. Spread a few spoonfuls of apple compote over the bottom of each tartlet shell. Arrange the apple slices overlapping on top, then sprinkle them with sugar. Bake the tartlets on the baking sheet in the heated oven until the rim of the pastry and the apples begin to turn golden, about 20 minutes. If you like, broil the apple tartlets as directed. Leave the tartlets to cool as directed, then carefully unmold them.

4 Make the apricot glaze and glaze the tartlets as directed.

FRENCH KNOW–HOW

The French countryside offers an abundance of fresh produce, fine cheeses, and a wide range of meats and poultry. Using a few basic techniques and a handful of traditional recipes, the cook is able to transform these ingredients into the refined yet simple dishes that are handed down from generation to generation.

EQUIPMENT

You won't find much specialized equipment in a French country kitchen because cooks rely on traditional tools. The first essential is a sharp chef's knife for chopping or cutting up meat and poultry, plus one or two smaller knives for vegetables. Keep them sharpened regularly with a steel or stone, and store them carefully so that the blades are not damaged. A whisk is often called for, to blend sauces to silky smoothness, or to whisk a batter or egg whites. Other standard kitchen equipment includes a vegetable peeler, a grater, and a citrus juicer, as well as wooden spoons for stirring and slotted spoons for lifting foods from liquid or fat. You will also need a colander, a strainer, and a rubber spatula.

There are a few tarts and quiches in this book, calling for a rolling pin and a heavy baking sheet that does not warp, as well as a tart pan, either fluted or plain, with a removable base. It is not advisable to change the size of the pan called for in any of these recipes because the proportions of pastry and filling will be wrong.

The country terrine is baked in a long, straight-sided terrine mold with a lid. For crêpes, a small frying pan works well if you don't have a traditional crêpe pan. A large sauté pan or a frying pan, as well as a roasting pan, will also come in handy for many dishes. A shallow, oval or rectangular baking dish is much used in France for baking and browning gratins and stuffed crêpes. I like to choose an attractive dish that can be transferred from oven to table so that food can be served piping hot. Flameproof enameled cast iron, or plain white heatproof ceramic dishes are particularly popular. Choose a dish that has low sides so that the oven heat dries the topping and turns it a crispy golden brown. For braising chicken and rabbit or making a lamb stew, a heavy casserole with a tight-fitting lid and heatproof handles is essential – be sure the base is thick enough to prevent scorching during the slow cooking. It is important to remember that a pot or pan should fit its purpose.

You won't find a food processor in a traditional French kitchen, but, for some of the recipes in this book, it will save time in chopping and puréeing. A blender can be used instead, but the ingredients may need to be worked in batches. An electric mixer takes the hard work out of whisking cream and egg whites.

INGREDIENTS

Even the smallest French country town boasts a weekly open market. On a market day townspeople rise early to search for locally grown ingredients – a basket overflowing with fresh produce is on the arm of virtually every pedestrian. Because fresh ingredients are so accessible and of such high quality, meals are organized around what is seasonally available.

France is surrounded on three sides by sea, so it is hardly surprising that, from Brittany in the northwest to sunny Provence in the south, seafood is the focus of many menus. The recipes in this book for shrimp, scallops, sole, and sea bass are just a beginning. Poultry is often the focus of the midday meal. Here you'll find several ideas for chicken to be sautéed, or marinated and then simmered in a sauce, with more recipes for duck and Cornish hen. The four main meats, particularly pork, are also common choices, often simmered until tender with vegetables, wine, and stock in a rich stew.

Vegetables do not just act as accompaniments in French cooking, they play a vital role in flavoring all manner of dishes. Most important is the allium family – onion, garlic, leeks, and shallots. Carrots and celery are a close second, with tomatoes, mushrooms, potatoes, and other roots as common additions. The south revels in vine-ripened tomatoes, bell peppers, eggplant, and zucchini, while in Burgundy wild mushrooms are so common in the autumn that it is not unusual to see whole families combing the woods for the precious fungi.

Depending on the season, you may find fruit paired with savory dishes as a foil to a piquant sauce. In autumn, duck is often matched with pears, while earlier in the year the choice may be fresh cherries. Fresh fruit is also a favorite ending to a

meal, particularly in summer. In winter, dried and fresh fruits such as apples frequently appear as desserts, baked into tarts and cakes. Dairy products are a mainstay of the French kitchen, with butter adding characteristic flavor to sauces such as *beurre blanc*, or binding flour in a flaky pastry shell. Stiff, nutty-flavored crème fraîche is frequently stirred into a savory sauce, with whipped sweetened Chantilly cream an essential component in many desserts. However, flavored oils should not be overlooked. In a broad belt running along the Mediterranean, olive oil is the cooking fat of choice, while walnut, hazelnut and other nut oils are favored inland. In southwestern France, you'll come across goose fat in dessert pastries as well as in savory dishes.

Parsley, thyme, rosemary, tarragon, and chervil are the common herbs in a French kitchen, often growing freely in the back yard. The fragrant leaves may be stirred into a recipe at the last minute to release fresh flavor and color, or added at the beginning of cooking so as to blend and marry with other ingredients. Perhaps the most basic ingredient of all is stock, often called the foundation of French cooking. Beef, veal, or chicken stock may be added after roasting to deglaze a pan to make gravy, or to provide the basis for a soup, sauce, or stew.

BEEF OR VEAL STOCK

🍴 MAKES 2 – 3 QUARTS

🥣 WORK TIME 20 – 30 MINUTES

🍲 COOKING TIME 4 – 5 HOURS

SHOPPING LIST

4 ½ lb	beef or veal bones, cut into pieces
2	onions, peeled and quartered
2	carrots, peeled and quartered
2	celery stalks, quartered
1	large bouquet garni
10	black peppercorns
1 tbsp	tomato paste

1 Heat the oven to 450°F. Roast the bones in a large pan until well browned, stirring occasionally, 30–40 minutes. Add the vegetables and brown, 15–20 minutes.

2 Transfer the bones and vegetables to a stockpot. Discard the fat from the pan, pour in 2 cups water, and bring to a boil, stirring. Add to the stockpot with the remaining ingredients and 3 ½ quarts water. Simmer, uncovered, skimming occasionally and adding water, if needed, 4–5 hours. Strain, then boil to concentrate the flavor, if you like. Cool, discard the fat, and refrigerate.

FISH STOCK

🍴 MAKES ABOUT 1 QUART

🥣 WORK TIME 10 – 15 MINUTES

🍲 COOKING TIME 20 MINUTES

SHOPPING LIST

1 lb	bones and heads of lean white fish, cut into 2-inch pieces
1	onion, thinly sliced
1 cup	dry white wine
3–5	sprigs of parsley
1 tsp	peppercorns

1 Wash the fish bones and heads; place them in a medium saucepan with the remaining ingredients.

2 Pour in 1 quart water and bring to a boil. Simmer, skimming occasionally with a large metal spoon, 20 minutes.

3 Strain the stock into a bowl. Cool, then cover, and keep in the refrigerator.

CHICKEN STOCK

🍴 MAKES ABOUT 2 QUARTS

🥣 WORK TIME 15 MINUTES

🍲 COOKING TIME UP TO 3 HOURS

SHOPPING LIST

2–2 ½ lb	chicken backs and necks
1	onion, quartered
1	carrot, quartered
1	celery stalk, quartered
1	bouquet garni
5	peppercorns

1 Put the chicken pieces into a large stockpot with the remaining ingredients.

2 Pour in 2 quarts water and bring to a boil. Simmer up to 3 hours, skimming occasionally with a large metal spoon, and adding more water if needed.

3 Strain the stock into a large bowl. Cool, then cover, and keep in the refrigerator.

TECHNIQUES

The French start with good ingredients, then treat them with care in the kitchen. Particular attention is paid to basic techniques, like slicing a vegetable correctly, or simmering a soup at just the right speed. Throughout this book, there are illustrations of basic processes, such as browning poultry, pork, or lamb to enhance their flavor, making a roux by cooking butter with flour to thicken a sauce, and sautéing a wide range of ingredients from mushrooms to chicken. Several of the recipes use less common ingredients, such as rabbit and duck, and you'll see how to prepare them, too.

Cooking methods in this book are equally varied, ranging from roasting meat in Leg of Lamb with Roasted Garlic and Shallots and pan-frying steak in Steak au Poivre to preparing and cooking a whole fish in Roast Sea Bass with Herb Butter Sauce. Braising, simmering, and deep-frying are still more techniques with which you will become familiar. You will learn how to make and bake sweet and savory pastry doughs, how to fry crêpes, and how to whip egg whites and poach them into light meringues. Turning to sauces, you will find out how to combine egg yolks, sugar, and milk to make vanilla custard sauce – also the base for ice cream. Preparing a simple cream sauce, or the more delicate *beurre blanc* or butter sauce, is made easy.

As with other volumes in the *Look & Cook* series, basic techniques that are commonly used in the recipes are described in detail. You will see how to chop herbs; how to peel, seed, and chop tomatoes; how to chop and slice onions; how to core and seed bell peppers and cut them into strips or dice; how to make chicken, beef, veal, and fish stock; how to make a bouquet garni; and how to peel and chop garlic.

MICROWAVE

To speed preparation, some of these recipes can be adapted for microwave cooking, especially when simmering or roasting is involved. For instance, to shorten the simmering time for Spring Lamb Stew, brown the cubes of lamb on top of the stove, then finish cooking the dish in the microwave. Marinate and brown the rabbit as directed for Rabbit with Provençal Herbs and Baked Tomatoes, then finish cooking the rabbit in the microwave. The microwave speeds the lengthy cooking time for Golden Rice Pudding: prepare the ingredients as directed and cook the rice pudding in the microwave. Keep careful watch, however, stirring often for even cooking.

Vegetables cook quickly and easily in the microwave, and because many of these recipes are based on, or filled with, vegetables, it proves a useful tool. For example, cook the spinach and mushrooms for Spinach and Mushroom Gratin in the microwave, transfer them to a baking dish, add the remaining ingredients, and brown in a conventional oven. The bell pepper and onion garnish for Omelet with Peppers and Tomatoes cooks in minutes in a microwave. Stir it into the egg mixture and finish the omelet on top of the stove. Cook the leeks for the Leek and Cheese Quiche in the microwave, set them in the tart shell with the custard and cheese, and bake in a conventional oven.

The microwave is also helpful in preparing certain basic ingredients. For example, it can ease the peeling of small onions or shallots. Trim 3 oz small onions or shallots, put them into a microwave-safe bowl and heat on High (100% power), 45 seconds, then squeeze each stalk end until the onions or shallots pop out of the skins. You can also cook bacon and melt chocolate in the microwave. For all recipes, be sure to follow manufacturers' instructions for cooking speeds and times.

CHEESE IN FRENCH COUNTRY COOKING

Cheese, notably Gruyère and Parmesan, has its place in French cooking, but by far the most cheese is eaten at the table as a separate course. It may appear before dessert, or be paired with fruit and replace dessert altogether.

A platter of cheeses should be a well-balanced contrast of appearance, taste, and texture. I usually choose one hard cheese such as Gruyère or Comté, one blue – bleu d'Auvergne is my favorite, but Roquefort is more common – and one soft, perhaps a wedge of Brie or Pont l'Evêque. There's a huge choice. A round or log of goat cheese is also a common addition. Just to remind you, France is said to have 365 cheeses, one for every day of the year.

Ripeness is most important when selecting cheese, and both odor and appearance are good tests. Hard, aged cheeses should smell nutty, almost spicy, as you hope they will taste, while softer, high-fat cheeses should be aromatic and some even quite pungent. No cheese, however, should be so overripe that it smells of ammonia. Look at the rind of the cheese as well. On hard and blue cheeses the rind should be firm and crusty, but with soft cheese this may indicate that it has been kept too long.

When serving a cheese course, arrange the wedges or rounds on a wooden board or a large, flat decorative plate. Best of all is a flat basket tray lined with edible leaves, such as grape leaves, or with paper napkins or doilies. The cheeses should all be at room temperature, accompanied by the bread of your choice. Nut or raisin breads are particularly good. When slicing the cheese, be sure to cut through the rind so each diner is served a piece of the rind as well as the desirable soft interior.

FRENCH COUNTRY COOKING AND YOUR HEALTH

Regardless of the style of cooking, variety and moderation are the key to a sensible diet. Variety in French country cooking is easy to achieve, given the wide range of ingredients traditionally used. Be sure to follow the French example of cooking with only the freshest and best-quality products.

If fat and calories are a concern, look to recipes where little fat is used in the cooking process, such as roasting, simmering, and sautéing. Leg of Lamb with Roasted Garlic and Shallots, Chicken with Provençal Herbs and Garlic Potatoes, and Scallops with Tomatoes, Garlic, and Herbs are all good examples. Serve the main course with grains and simply garnished vegetables.

To moderate your cholesterol intake, choose dishes in which saturated fat can easily be replaced or eliminated. Use olive or canola oil in place of butter when sautéing the mushrooms in Warm Salad of Wild Mushrooms. With Roast Sea Bass, use only olive oil in the Herb Butter Sauce, or omit the sauce altogether. In other recipes, fat, calories, and cholesterol can be further reduced by omitting some ingredients completely. Bacon, cream, and cheese fall into this category.

Always consider the meal as a whole. Plan balanced menus using a healthful variety of fresh seasonal foods and cooking methods.

HOW-TO BOXES

In each of the recipes in **French Country Cooking** *you'll find pictures of all the techniques used. However, some basic preparations appear in a number of recipes, and these are shown in extra detail in these special "how-to" boxes:*

INDEX

ACKNOWLEDGMENTS

Photographers' Assistants Nick Allen and Sid Sideris

Chef Eric Treuille
Home Economist Maddalena Bastianelli

US Editors Julee Binder and Constance Mersel

Typesetting Rowena Feeny and Axis Design

Text film by Disc to Print (UK) Limited

Production Consultant Lorraine Baird

*Anne Willan would like to thank her chief editor
Jacqueline Bobrow and associate editor Valerie Cipollone
for their vital help with writing this book and researching
and testing the recipes, aided by Brenda Garza, Karen Ryan,
and La Varenne chefs and trainees.*

WEIGHTS AND MEASURES

MEASUREMENT CONVERSIONS

US Cups	Metric
1 tbsp	15 ml
1/8 cup	30 ml
1/4 cup	60 ml
3/8 cup	90 ml
1/2 cup	125 ml
2/3 cup	150 ml
3/4 cup	175 ml
1 cup (1/2 pint)	250 ml
1 1/4 cups	300 ml
1 1/2 cups	375 ml
2 cups (1 pint)	500 ml
2 1/2 cups	600 ml
3 3/4 cups	900 ml
1 qt (4 cups)	1 litre
1 1/4 quarts	1.25 litres
3 US pints	1.5 litres
2 quarts	2 litres

Standards

1 tsp = 5 ml
1 tbsp = 15 ml
1 fl oz = 30 ml
1 ml = 0.035 fl oz
1 UK pint = 20 fl oz
1 US pint = 16 fl oz
1 litre = 33 fl oz
      (1 US qt)

Length Conversions

1 cm = 0.3 in

SOLID WEIGHT CONVERSIONS

US	Metric
1/2 oz	15 g
1 oz	30 g
2 oz	60 g
3 oz	90 g
4 oz (1/4 lb)	120 g
5 oz	150 g
6 oz	180 g
8 oz (1/2 lb)	240 g
12 oz (3/4 lb)	360 g
1 lb (16 oz)	480 g

Standards

1 oz = 30 g   1 lb = 16 oz (480 g)
1 g = 0.35 oz   1 kg = 2.2 lb

OVEN TEMPERATURE CONVERSIONS

°F	Gas	°C
225	1/4	110
250	1/2	120
275	1	140
300	2	150
325	3	160
350	4	175
375	5	190
400	6	200
425	7	220
450	8	230
475	9	240
500	10	260